Student's Book

Stage 5

English in a quarter of the time!

The Callan ® Method was first developed and published
in 1960 by R.K. T. Callan.

First edition by R. K. T. Callan, published for the international market in 2012
This second edition by R. K. T. Callan, published for the international market in 2013

Student's Book – Stage 5
978-1-78229-240-1

Printed in the EU

Published by

CALLAN METHOD ORGANISATION LTD.
702, The Chandlery, 50 Westminster Bridge Road, London, SE1 7QY

www.callan.co.uk

- Para obtener la traducción de este prefacio en español, visitar www.callan.co.uk/preface/es
- Per una traduzione di questa prefazione in Italiano, visitare il sito www.callan.co.uk/preface/it
- Para obter uma tradução deste prefácio em português, visite www.callan.co.uk/preface/pt
- Z polskim tłumaczeniem tego wstępu można zapoznać się na stronie www.callan.co.uk/preface/pl
- Pour obtenir la traduction de cette préface en français, rendez-vous sur le site www.callan.co.uk/preface/fr
- Bu önsözün Türkçe çevirisi için aşağıdaki web adresini ziyaret edin www.callan.co.uk/preface/tr
- 本序言的中文翻译，请访问 www.callan.co.uk/preface/ch
- 前書きの日本語版の翻訳は次ページをご覧ください www.callan.co.uk/preface/jp
- للاطلاع على ترجمة هذه المقدمة باللغة العربية يرجى زيارة www.callan.co.uk/preface/ar

Welcome to the Callan Method

Learning English with the Callan™ Method is fast and effective!

The Callan Method is a teaching method created specifically to improve your English in an intensive atmosphere. The teacher is constantly asking questions, so you are hearing and using the language as much as possible. When you speak in the lesson, the teacher corrects your grammar and pronunciation mistakes, and you learn a lot from this correction.

The Callan Method teaches English vocabulary and grammar in a carefully programmed way, with systematic revision and reinforcement. In the lesson, there is a lot of speaking and listening practice, but there is also reading and writing so that you revise and consolidate what you have learned.

With the Callan Method, the teacher speaks quickly so that you learn to understand English when it is spoken at natural speed. This also means that everyone is concentrating hard all the time.

English in a quarter of the time

The Callan Method can teach English in a quarter of the time taken by any other method on the market. Instead of the usual 350 hours necessary to get the average student to the level of the Cambridge Preliminary English Test (PET), the Callan Method can take as little as 80 hours, and only 160 hours for the Cambridge First Certificate in English (FCE).

The method is suitable for students of all nationalities, and ages. It requires no equipment (not even a whiteboard) or other books, and can be used for classes at private schools, state schools and universities. It is also possible for students to use the books to practise with each other when they are not at school.

In addition to this, students can practise their English online using the interactive exercises, which are available to students who study at licensed schools. Ask your school for details.

The Callan Method in practice

A Callan Method English lesson is probably very different from lessons you have done in the past. You do not sit in silence, doing a reading comprehension test or a grammar exercise from a book. You do not have 'free conversation', where you only use the English you already feel comfortable with. Of course, activities like this can help you, but you can do them at home with a book, or in a coffee bar. In a Callan Method lesson, you are busy with important activities that you cannot do outside the classroom. You are listening to English all the time. You are speaking English a lot, and all your mistakes are corrected. You learn quickly because you are always surrounded by English. There is no silence and no time to get bored or lose your concentration. And it is also fun!

So, what exactly happens in a Callan Method lesson, and how does it work?

The teacher asks you questions

The Callan Method books are full of questions. Each question practises a word, an expression, or a piece of grammar. The teacher is standing, and asks the questions to the students one by one. You never know when the teacher will ask you, so you are always concentrating. When one student finishes answering one question, the teacher immediately starts to ask the next question.

The teacher speaks quickly

The teacher in a Callan Method lesson speaks quickly. This is because, in the real world, it is natural to speak quickly. If you want to understand normal English, you must practise listening to quick natural speech and become able to understand English without first translating into your language. This idea of not translating is at the centre of the Callan Method; this method helps you to start thinking in English.

Also, we do not want you to stop and think a lot about the grammar while you are speaking. We want you to speak as a reflex, instinctively. And do not worry about mistakes. You will, naturally, make a lot of mistakes in the lessons, but Callan Method teachers correct your mistakes, and you learn from the corrections. When you go home, of course it will help if you read your book, think about the grammar, study the vocabulary, and do all the things that language students do at home – but the lessons are times to practise your listening and speaking, with your books closed!

The teacher says every question twice, and helps you with the answer

In the lesson, the teacher speaks quickly, so we say the questions twice. This way, you have another chance to listen if you did not understand everything the first time.

The teacher then immediately says the beginning of the answer. This is to help you (and 'push' you) to start speaking immediately. So, for example:

Teacher: *"Are there two chairs in this room? Are there two chairs in this room? No, there aren't ..."*

Student (immediately): *"No, there aren't two chairs in this room; there are twelve chairs in this room."*

If the teacher does not 'push' you by giving you the beginning of the answer, you might start to think too much, and translate into your language.

The teacher will speak along with you all the time while you are saying your answer. So, if you forget a word or you are not sure what to say, you will always hear the next word or two from the teacher. You should repeat after the teacher, but immediately try again to continue with the answer yourself. You must always try to continue speaking, and only copy the teacher when you cannot continue alone. That way, you will become more confident and learn more quickly. Never simply wait for help from the teacher and then copy – you will not improve so quickly.

Long answers, with the same grammar as the question

We want you to practise your speaking as much as possible, so you always make complete sentences when you speak in the lesson, using the same grammatical structure as in the question. For example:

Teacher: *"About how many pages are there in this book?"*

Student: *"There are about two hundred pages in that book."*

In this way, you are not just answering a question; you are making full sentences with the vocabulary and the grammar that you need to learn.

Correction by imitation

With the Callan Method, the teacher corrects all your mistakes the moment you make them. The teacher corrects you by imitating (copying) your mistake and then saying the correct pronunciation/form of the word. For example, if you say "He come from Spain", the teacher quickly says "not come - ***comes***". This correction by imitation helps you to hear the difference between your mistake and the proper English form. You should immediately repeat the correct word and continue with your sentence. You learn a lot from this correction of your mistakes, and constant correction results in fast progress.

Contracted forms

In the lesson, the teacher uses contractions (e.g. the teacher says "I don't" instead of "I do not"). This is because it is natural to use contractions in spoken English and you must learn to understand them. Also, if you want to sound natural when you speak, you must learn to use contractions.

Lesson structure

Every school is different, but a typical 50-minute Callan lesson will contain about 35 minutes of speaking, a 10-minute period for reading, and a 5-minute dictation. The reading practice and the dictation are often in the middle of the lesson.

In the reading part, you read and speak while the teacher helps you and corrects your mistakes. In the dictation, you practise your writing, but you are also listening to the teacher. So, a 50-minute Callan lesson is 50 minutes of spoken English with no silence!

No chatting

Although the Callan Method emphasises the importance of speaking practice, this does not mean chatting (free conversation). You learn English quickly with the Callan Method partly because the lessons are organised, efficient, fast and busy. There is no time wasted on chatting; this can be done before or after the lesson.

Chatting is not a good way to spend your time in an English lesson. First, only some of the students speak. Second, in a chat, people only use the English that they already know. Third, it is difficult for a teacher to correct mistakes during a conversation.

The Callan Method has none of these problems. All through the lesson, every student is listening and speaking, practising different vocabulary and structures, and learning from the correction of their mistakes. And nobody has time to get bored!

Repeat, repeat, repeat!

Systematic revision

In your native language, you sometimes read or hear a word that you do not already know. You usually need to read or hear this new word only once or twice in order to remember it and then use it yourself. However, when you are learning a foreign language, things are very different. You need to hear, see and use words and grammatical structures many times before you really know them properly. So your studies must involve a system of revision (repeating what you have studied before). This is absolutely essential. If there is no system of revision in your studies, you will forget what you have studied and will not be able to speak or understand better than before.

In every Callan Method lesson, of course you learn new English, practise it, and progress through your book. However, you also do a lot of revision so that you can really learn what you have studied. Your teacher can decide how much revision your class needs, but it will always be an important part of your studies.

Also, because there is a lot of revision, it is not important for you to understand everything the first time; it gets easier. The revision with Callan is automatic and systematic. Every day you do a lot of revision and then learn some new English.

Revision in reading and dictation too

The reading and dictation practice in the lessons is part of Callan's systematic revision as well. First, you learn a new word in the speaking part of the lesson; a few lessons later, you meet it again when you are reading; finally, the word appears in a dictation. This is all written into the Callan Method; it happens automatically.

Correcting your dictations

With the Callan Method, there is little or no homework to do, but it is very important that you correct your dictations. These are printed in your book and so you can easily correct them at home, on the bus, or wherever. It is important to do this because it helps you to learn the written forms of the words you have already studied in earlier lessons.

Your first lessons with the Callan Method

During your first lesson with the Callan Method, all of the questions and some of the vocabulary are new for you; you have not done any revision yet. For this reason, the teacher may not ask you many questions. You can sit and listen, and become more familiar with the method - the speed, the questions, the correction etc.

History of the Callan Method – Robin Callan

Robin Callan, who passed away in April 2014, was the creator of the Callan Method. In addition to owning the Callan School in London's Oxford Street, he also ran Callan Method Organisation Ltd. This company, now managed by a dedicated team of Callan Method professionals, continues to grow, supplying Callan Method books to schools all over the world.

Robin Callan grew up in Ely, Cambridgeshire, England. In his early twenties, he went to Italy to teach English in Salerno. Although he enjoyed teaching, Robin thought that the way in which teachers were expected to teach their lessons was inefficient and boring. He became very interested in the mechanisms of language learning, and was sure that he could radically improve the way English was taught.

He remained in Italy and started to write his own books for teaching English. He used these in his own classes and, over the following ten years, gained an immense amount of practical experience and a reputation for teaching English quickly and effectively.

When he returned to England, he opened his school in Oxford Street. As the Method became more and more popular with students, the school grew and moved to larger premises. Robin continued to write his Callan Method books, and today the Method is used by schools all over the world.

Robin Callan was always passionate about English literature, especially poetry. For this reason, he bought The Orchard Tea Garden in Grantchester, near Cambridge, which attracts thousands of tourists each year. Throughout the 20th century, it was a popular meeting place for many famous Cambridge University students and important figures from English literature, such as Rupert Brooke, Virginia Woolf and E.M. Forster. Today, it is also home to the Rupert Brooke Museum.

Mr Callan lived in Grantchester for many years, and played an active role in the management of his companies well into his retirement and old age. He left an amazing legacy on which we all continue to build.

How Callan Method Stages compare to CEFR* levels and University of Cambridge General English exams

** Common European Framework of Reference*

It is difficult to compare the Callan Method books directly with the CEFR levels and Cambridge exams, but below is an approximate guide.

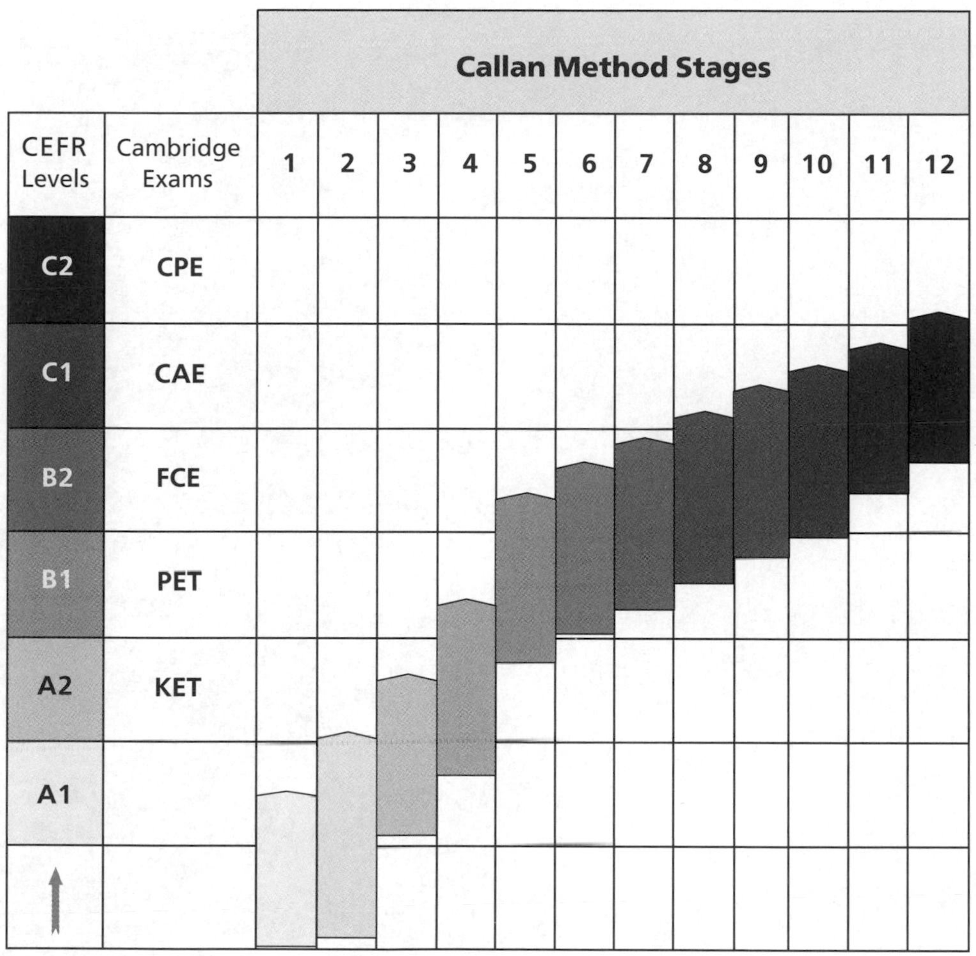

www.callan.co.uk

STAGE 5

LESSON 61

315 **chat** **online**

Do you prefer chatting with your friends on the phone or online?

I prefer chatting with my friends ...

Why?

How often do you go online to look at your email?

I go online ... to look at my email

notice

Do you notice anything different about the classroom today?

Yes, I notice something different ... ~ No, I don't notice anything different ...

What's the first thing you notice about people when you meet them for the first time?

The first thing I notice about people when I meet them for the first time is their voice (clothes, eyes etc.)

free **busy**

Are most people busy on Sunday?

No, most people aren't ...; they're free

What do we mean by a free meal?

By a free meal, we mean that we don't have to pay for it

Do you believe that the best things in life are free?

Yes, I believe ... ~ No, I don't believe ...

316 **lie** **comfortable** **uncomfortable**

pillow

Is the book standing on the table?

No, the book isn't standing ...; it's lying ...

Is it more comfortable to sleep lying down or sitting up?

It's more comfortable to sleep lying down than sitting up

Do you find it comfortable to sleep without a pillow?

Yes, I find it ... ~ No, I don't find it ...; I find it uncomfortable

wake up – woke up – woken up

go to sleep **immediately** **midnight**

Do you usually go to sleep before midnight?

Yes, I usually ... ~ No, I don't usually ...

Do you generally wake up early?

Yes, I generally ... ~ No, I don't generally ...

What are the three forms of "wake up"?

The three forms of "wake up" are "wake up, woke up, woken up"

What was the first thing you saw when you woke up today?

The first thing I saw when I woke up ...

Have you ever woken up too late to go to school (or work)?

Yes, I've sometimes woken up ... ~ No, I've never woken up ...

317 **through** **button** **buttonhole**

What am I doing?

You're putting your pen through the buttonhole in your shirt (blouse etc.)

When you look through your bedroom window, what do you see?

When I look through my bedroom window, I see ...

If you went from London to Rome, which cities would you perhaps have to go through?

If I went ..., I would perhaps have to go through Paris, Milan etc.

career

Would you like a career in the army?

Yes, I'd like ... ~ No, I wouldn't like ...

cross **crossroads** **test**

What's this?

It's a cross

When a teacher puts a cross next to an answer in a written test, what does it mean?

When a teacher ..., it means the answer is wrong

Are there any crossroads at the end of the street where you live?

Yes, there are some ... where I live ~ No, there aren't any ... where I live

318 **danger** **dangerous** **dangerously**

alcohol **detective**

What colour do we use for danger?

We use red for danger

Is it dangerous to drive after drinking alcohol?

Yes, it's dangerous ...

Would you like to live dangerously like a detective: somebody like Sherlock Holmes, for example?

Yes, I'd like ... ~ No, I wouldn't like ...

should **obligation** **alternative**

ambulance

The sentences "I must study" and "I should study" are not the same. The first sentence, "I must study", means that I have an obligation to study; I have no alternative. The second sentence, "I should study", means that I have alternatives; I can go to the cinema if I like, or for a walk, but studying is the right thing for me to do. The best idea is to study.

What's the difference between these two sentences: "I must study" and "I should study"?

The difference between those two sentences is that "I must study" means that I have no alternative, whereas "I should study" means I have alternatives but that studying is the right thing for me to do

How do we translate "I must study"?

We translate "I must study" with ...

And how do we translate "I should study"?

We translate "I should study" with ...

319 Do you think people should be more polite in the shops and streets?

Yes, I think ...

Do you agree that students should study hard?

Yes, I agree ...

Do you agree that young people should help the old? Yes, I agree ...

What should we do when somebody is dangerously ill? When somebody ..., we should immediately call an ambulance

What do you think you should do if you want to make a lot of money? If you want to ..., I think you should ...

correct **grammatical**

Do you correct your dictations during the lesson? Yes, I correct my dictations ... ~ No, I don't correct my dictations ...; I correct them after the lesson

In a Callan Method lesson, does the teacher correct your grammatical mistakes? Yes, in a Callan Method lesson, ...

How can we correct our mistakes in our pronunciation? We can correct ... by listening and speaking as much as possible

problem **cause** **colleague** **boss**

freedom **justice**

If you have a problem with a colleague at work, should you speak to your boss about it? Yes, if I have ..., I should speak to my boss about it

320 Can smoking cause health problems? Yes, smoking can ...

In history, have many people died for the causes of freedom and justice? Yes, in history, many people ...

as

As we have now studied about a thousand words and a lot of the grammar, can you hold a simple conversation in English? Yes, as we have ..., I can hold ...

As you are not tall enough to reach the ceiling, what would you have to do if you wanted to reach it? As I am not ..., I would have to put a chair on the table and stand on the chair if I wanted ...

that is

We use the words "that is" when we want to correct something we have just said, or when we want to add more information.

Give me a sentence with "that is" in it.

Everybody loves that film; that is, everybody I've spoken to. We will go to the cinema this evening; that is, if we have enough money

bone

Have you ever broken any of the bones in your body?

Yes, I've broken one/some of ... ~ No, I've never broken any of ...

When? How?

321 *Dictation 36*

If somebody wants/ to buy my motorbike/ before I go away,/ I'll sell it/ for almost nothing./ It is worth paying a little more,/ and going to a good hairdresser./ Parents often read/ bedtime stories to their children./ In some ways,/ life today is harder/ than it was in the past,/ but in other ways/ it is easier./ The waiter brought us the menu,/ but it was the waitress/ who brought the food.

LESSON 62

322 **life** **lives** **the poor** **the rich**

If a noun finishes with "f" or "fe", we make the plural by changing the "f" or "fe" to "ves". For example, the plural of "wife" is "wives"; the plural of "knife" is "knives"; the plural of "scarf" is "scarves".

What's the plural of "life"?
The plural of ...

Do you think the lives of the poor are happier than those of the rich?
Yes, I think ... ~ No, I don't think ...; I think they're less happy

although

Make a sentence with the word "although" in it.
Although the food was not very nice, I ate it because I was hungry

Although you're now able to hold a simple conversation in English, do you think you should keep studying?
Yes, although I'm ..., I think I should ...

Are some people always happy although they have problems in their lives?
Yes, some people ...

cook **tasty** **pasta**

Is there a restaurant near here that cooks tasty food?
Yes, there's a ... ~ No, there isn't a ...

Is it difficult to cook pasta?
No, it isn't difficult ...; it's easy

323 Are you a good cook?
Yes, I'm a good cook ~ No, I'm not a good cook

independent

Do you think that all the countries of the world should be independent?
Yes, I think ... ~ No, I don't think ...

origin

Do many European languages have their origins in Latin?

Yes, many European languages ...

belong to

Why don't you take this book home with you after the lesson?

I don't take that book home with me ... because it doesn't belong to me

Who does that pen belong to?

This pen belongs to me

If a factory belonged to you, do you think you would be able to make a lot of money?

Yes, if a factory belonged to me, I think I would be able ...

could vice versa

"Could" is the past of "can", but we can also use "could" instead of "would be able" in conditional sentences.

What can we use instead of "would be able" in conditional sentences?

We can use "could" instead of ...

Give me an example, please.

If I was a bird, I could fly

324 Now I'm going to ask you some questions with "could" and you answer with "would be able", and vice versa.

If you were very, very tall, could you touch the ceiling?

Yes, if I were ..., would be able to touch ...

If you were a doctor, would you be able to help people who were ill?

Yes, if I were ..., I could help ...

If you were as strong as a horse, could you lift a man above your head with only one hand?

Yes, if I were ..., I would be able to lift a man above my head ...

throw

What am I going to do?

You're going to throw your pen at the window

Do you think you could throw a stone further than I can? Yes, I think I could ... further than you can
~ No, I don't think I could ... further than you can

alive dead

Is Napoleon alive? No, Napoleon isn't alive; he's dead

drop go without

What am I doing? You're dropping your pen on the table

What's the pen doing? The pen's dropping on the table

325 What would happen if I dropped a glass on the floor? If you dropped ..., it would break

What's the longest (time) you have ever gone without drinking a drop of water? The longest I've ever ... is ...

assassinate

What happened to President Kennedy? President Kennedy was assassinated (in 1963)

usual unusual

Did anything unusual happen to you yesterday? Yes, something unusual happened to me yesterday
~ No, nothing unusual happened to me yesterday

What?

Is it usual for people in your country to eat hot food for breakfast?
Yes, it's usual for people in my country ...
~ No, it isn't usual for people in my country ...

Is it unusual for children to find coffee tasty? Yes, it's unusual ...

still yet in progress

We use "still" for something that is in progress at the moment, whereas we use "yet" for something that has not begun or happened.

For example, "It is still winter; it isn't spring yet. It is still 20...; it isn't 20... yet. It is still Monday; it isn't Tuesday yet" etc.

We generally use "still" in positive sentences, whereas we generally use "yet" in questions and negative sentences, but not always. We must learn when to use "still" and when to use "yet" by practice.

326 What's the difference between "still" and "yet"?

The difference between "still" and "yet" is that we use "still" for something that is in progress at the moment, whereas we use "yet" for something that has not begun or happened. We generally use "still" in positive sentences, whereas we generally use "yet" in questions and negative sentences

Give me some examples, please.

It's still winter; it isn't spring yet

Has the lesson finished yet?

No, the lesson hasn't finished yet; it's still in progress

Have we finished speaking yet?

No, we haven't finished speaking yet; we're still speaking

Have they gone home yet?

No, they haven't gone home yet; they're still here

Has the spring (summer etc.) begun yet?

No, the spring (summer etc.) hasn't begun yet; it's still ...

Will I still be in this country in two weeks' time?

Yes, you'll still be ...

special

Dictation 37

If I receive a call from him,/ I'll stay./ It is an ordinary paint factory;/ it makes nothing special./ Rainy days make me sad./ I listened,/ but could hear no sound. What song do you suggest/ we get him to give us/ if he is not too tired?/ We don't turn right/ until we get to the next street./ The opposite of death is life.

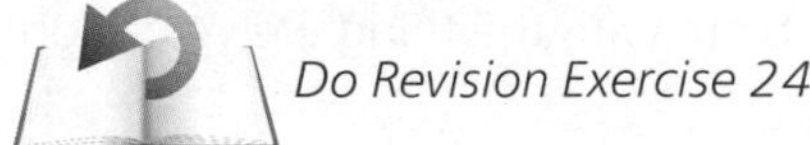

Do Revision Exercise 24

LESSON 63

327 **clean** **dirty** **dirt** **know of**

Are the bottoms of your shoes clean? No, the bottoms of my shoes aren't clean; they're dirty

When our shoes are dirty, what should we do? When our shoes are dirty, we should clean them

Which do you think is the cleanest city you know of? I think ... is the cleanest city I know of

And which do you think is the dirtiest? I think ... is the dirtiest

Which do you think is less unpleasant: the dirt of the city or the dirt of the country, of the farm etc.? I think the dirt of the ... is less unpleasant than the dirt of the ...

to be afraid

Do you remember if you were afraid of the dark when you were a little child? Yes, I remember I was afraid of the dark when I was a little child ~ No, I don't remember if I was afraid of the dark when I was a little child

Would you be afraid to go round the world in a small, open boat? Yes, I would be afraid ... ~ No, I wouldn't be afraid ...

Do people shake when they feel very afraid? Yes, people shake ...

328 **guard** **on your guard** **off your guard**

What's the best way to guard against becoming ill? The best way ... is to eat healthy food, sleep well and do exercise

Must we be on our guard when we buy something from a man selling things in the street? Yes, we must be ...

Why? Because maybe we won't be able to find him again if there's a problem with the thing we've bought

What's the opposite of "on your guard"? The opposite of "on your guard" is "off your guard"

calm **quietly**

What's the best way to calm somebody down when he's very angry? The best way ... is to speak quietly and pleasantly to him

Are we having calm weather at the moment? Yes, we're having ... ~ No, we aren't having ...

if I were **king**

person (1st, 2nd person etc.)

In the 2nd conditional, we can use the verb "to be" in the past simple and say "if I was", "if you were", "if he was" etc. or we can use "were" for all persons and say "if I were", "if you were", "if he were" etc. The second form is perhaps more common.

What are the two ways of forming the 2nd conditional with the verb "to be"? The two ways of forming the 2nd conditional with the verb "to be" are "if I was" and "if I were"

329 If you were a millionaire, where would you live? If I were ..., I would live in ...

Why?

If I were you, which language would I speak? If you were me, you would speak ...

If you were a king, what would your wife be called? If I were a king, my wife would be called a queen

If there wasn't a light in this room, would we be able to see well when it got dark? No, if there wasn't ..., we wouldn't ...; we would see badly

If there weren't any food in the world, would we all die? Yes, if there weren't ..., we would all die

If you weren't you, who would you like to be? If I weren't me, I would like to be ...

Why?

if I were you advice expression especially

We say "If I were you" when we want to give advice to somebody, especially when we think perhaps there is a problem. For example, "If I were you, I would go to see a doctor" or "I wouldn't open that door if I were you!"

Can we use the expression "if I were you" to give advice to somebody?
Yes, we can use the expression ...

Give me an example, please
"If I were you, I would eat more vegetables" or "I wouldn't buy that car if I were you!"

330 What's the biggest problem in your life at the moment?
The biggest problem in my life at the moment is ...

Give him/her some advice, please.
If I were you, I would ...

win – won – won lottery

What's another opposite of the verb "lose" besides "find"?
Another opposite ... is "win"

What are the three forms of "win"?
The three forms of "win" are "win, won, won"

Does your country usually win at football?
Yes, my country ... ~ No, my country ...; it usually loses

Do you do the lottery?
Yes, I do the lottery ~ No, I don't do the lottery

Have you ever won?
Yes, I've won ~ No, I've never won

If you won a million pounds, what would you do with it?
If I won ..., I would ...

useful useless possess

Is this pen useless?
No, this pen isn't useless; it's useful

What do we do with useless things?
We throw useless things away

What are the two most useful things you possess?
The two most useful things I possess are ...

331 **Do you think that what you're learning now will be useful to you later on in life?**

Yes, I think that what I'm learning now will be useful to me later on in life

Why?

Because it will help me get work, and speak to people from other countries

take by surprise

Dictation 38

In the struggle/ the enemy were surrounded/ at great speed/ and were taken by surprise/ without their swords/ in their hands./ I won't buy him/ a newspaper again./ Fetch me the salad bowl, please./ He is sorry that he sold his old house,/ which was in a quiet road./ The house he has now/ is in a very noisy street,/ and so he must try/ and find another,/ if possible.

LESSON 64

332 Contraction of "would" contract

The contraction of "I would" is "I'd". We can use contractions for all the persons and say "I'd", "you'd", "he'd", "she'd", "it'd", "we'd", "you'd", they'd".

What's the contraction of "I would"? — The contraction of ...

What are the contractions of "you would", "he would", "she would" etc.? — The contractions of "you would", "he would", "she would" etc. are "you'd", "he'd, "she'd", "it'd", "we'd", "you'd", "they'd"

From now on I want you to always use the contractions when speaking.

If you went to the cinema this evening, which film would you see? — If I went ..., I'd see ...

If I were you, which language would I speak? — If you were me, you'd speak ...

If a plant had no water, would it die? — Yes, if a plant ...

Contraction of "would" with other words

We can contract "would" with almost any word. For example, "the book would" becomes "the book'd"; "who would" becomes "who'd" etc.

What's the contraction of "book would"? — The contraction of "book would" is "book'd"

333 lesson would; who would; what would; which would — lesson'd; who'd; what'd; which'd

If you were a king, what'd your wife be called? — If I were a king, my wife'd be called a queen

If you lost your way in a large city, who'd you ask? — If I lost my way ..., I'd ask a policeman

If today were Sunday, what'd tomorrow be? — If today were Sunday, tomorrow'd be Monday

sandwich **cheese**

When office workers are too busy to leave their desks for lunch, do they often just have a quick sandwich? — Yes, when office workers ...

What kind of things do we put in sandwiches? — We put meat, cheese, egg etc. in sandwiches

fault **faultless** **faulty**

fix

What's your biggest fault? — My biggest fault is ...

If your computer was faulty, would you know how to fix the fault? — Yes, if my computer was faulty, I'd know ... ~ No, if my computer was faulty, I wouldn't know ...

Are your dictations usually faultless? — No, my dictations aren't usually faultless; they usually contain mistakes

If a student makes a mistake in his dictation, is it usually his fault or the teacher's fault? — If a student ..., it's usually his fault, but it could sometimes be the teacher's fault

334 **OK** **all right**

"OK" and "all right" have the same meaning.

What can we say instead of "OK"? — Instead of "OK" we can say "all right"

compare **comparison**

have something in common

Can we compare Michelangelo with Napoleon? — No, we can't compare ...

Why not? — Because they were two completely different kinds of people, who did different things from each other

What must two people or things have if we want to make a comparison between them? — If we want to make a comparison between two people or things, they must have something in common

ice **cool**

What do we use ice for?

We use ice for putting in drinks to cool them etc.

pour

What am I doing?

You're pouring some water (wine etc.) from a bottle into a glass

335 **unite**

Do you think that all the countries of the world will unite one day?

Yes, I think ... ~ No, I don't think ...

even **surprising**

The word "even" can have a similar meaning to "also", but we use it when the next piece of information is surprising.

Give me a sentence with "even" in it.

She speaks Russian, German, French, and even Chinese ~ He was very impolite; he didn't even say "hello" ~ It's very simple; even a child could understand it

mix **mixture** **pink**

Do we generally mix sugar with potatoes?

No, we don't generally ...

Do you think a mixture of tea and coffee would make a pleasant drink?

No, I don't think ...; it would make an unpleasant drink

If you mixed some red and white paint together, what would you get?

If I mixed ..., I'd get pink paint

care **care for** **take care of**

Who cared for you when you were a child?

My mother cared for me when I was a child

336 Do you think the young should take care of the old?

Yes, I think ...

Do you take good care of your health? Yes, I take good care of my health ~ No, I don't take good care of my health

Do you care what people think or say about you? Yes, I care ... about me ~ No, I don't care ... about me

appointment **keep an appointment** **hurry**

take your time

If you were late for a very important appointment, would you take your time? No, if I were ..., I wouldn't take my time; I'd hurry

Why? Because it's important to keep appointments that we've made

Why is it sometimes a bad thing to hurry? It's sometimes ... because we often make mistakes when we hurry

Would you take your time going home if somebody told you your house was on fire? No, I wouldn't take my time going home if somebody told me my house was on fire; I'd hurry

What's the translation of "I am in a hurry"? The translation of "I am in a hurry" is "..."

plenty of

The words "plenty of" mean "more than enough".

What do the words "plenty of" mean? The words "plenty of" ...

337 Do people hurry when they have plenty of time? No, people don't hurry ...; they take their time

What's the opposite of "plenty of water"? The opposite of "plenty of water" is "little water" or "not enough water"

Do Revision Exercise 25

LESSON 65

338 **for since period point**

We came into this room at (six o'clock). The time now is (half past six). Therefore, we have been in this room for (half an hour). We have been in this room since (six o'clock).

We use the word "for" when we say a period of time. For example, "for half an hour"; "for two weeks"; "for six months"; "for ten years" etc. We use the word "since" when we say the point at which the period began. For example, "since six o'clock"; "since last Monday"; "since January"; "since 2002" etc.

What's the difference between "for" and "since"?

The difference between "for" and "since" is that we use the word "for" when we say a period of time, whereas we use the word "since" when we say the point at which the period began

Give me some examples of "for".

for half an hour; for two weeks

Now give me some examples of "since".

since six o'clock; since last June

How long have you been in this room for?

I've been in this room for ...

Since when has he/she been in this room?

He's/She's been in this room since ...

How long have you lived in this town for?

I've lived in this town for ...

Since when has he/she lived in this town?

He's/She's lived in this town since ...

339 About how long have you known me for?

I've known you for about ...

Since when has he/she known me?

He's/She's known you since ...

Have you been able to speak English for more than ten years?

Yes, I've been able to ... ~ No, I haven't been able to ...

Have you been able to speak English since you were a young child?

Yes, I've ... since I was ... ~ No, I haven't ... since I was ...

kitchen fridge freezer cooker

sink microwave

What kind of things does a kitchen usually contain?

A kitchen usually contains a fridge, a freezer, a cooker, a sink etc.

Does meat last longer in a fridge or a freezer?

Meat lasts longer ...

Why do some people like using microwaves?

Some people ... because they cook food very quickly

studies

Did you find English pronunciation a little difficult at the beginning of your studies?

Yes, I found ... of my studies

Do you hope your English studies will help your future career?

Yes, I hope my ... my future career

340 **lend – lent – lent return**

Would you lend me some money if I asked you?

Yes, I'd lend you some money if you asked me ~ No, I wouldn't lend you any money if you asked me

If you lent something to somebody and they didn't return it, what'd you do?

If I lent something ..., I'd ...

first name surname

What's your first name?

My first name's ...

What's your surname?

My surname's ...

actor actress famous film star

Would you like to be famous?
Yes, I'd like ...
~ No, I wouldn't like ...

What's a film star?
A film star is a famous actor or actress in the cinema world

Tell me the names of some famous film stars, please.
Johnny Depp, Penelope Cruz etc.

Name a few famous people in history?
A few famous people in history are Shakespeare, Einstein, Michelangelo etc.

341 **industrial agricultural region**

What's the most industrial city in your country?
... is the most industrial city in my country

What's the most agricultural region of your country?
... is the most agricultural region of my country

apologize apology

keep somebody waiting

What do we say when we apologize for doing something wrong?
When we apologize ..., we say "I'm sorry"

If you keep somebody waiting for a long time, should you apologize?
Yes, if you keep ..., you should apologize

What's the noun of the verb "apologize"?
The noun ... is "apology"

avoid

How can we help to avoid becoming ill?
We can help ... by living a healthy life

bend

Do you have to bend down if you want to touch your feet?
No, I don't ... if I want to touch my feet, but it would be the easiest way

342 **century**

Which do you think was the best century in history to live in?

I think the ... century was the best ...

fashion

Do you like the fashion in clothes at the moment?

Yes, I like ... ~ No, I don't like ...

gate

Does this school have a gate outside it?

Yes, this school has ... ~ No, this school doesn't have ...

worry **be worried**

Do some people worry too much?

Yes, some people ...

Are you worried about your future?

Yes, I'm worried about my future ~ No, I'm not worried about my future

Why should you not worry if you don't immediately understand some of the grammar in this book?

I shouldn't worry if I don't ... because I will practise it again in other lessons, and I can study it at home

run

When we're in a hurry, what must we do?

When we're ..., we must run

343 **What's the furthest you've ever run?**

The furthest I've ever run is ...

Dictation 39

Comedy films make us laugh./ He won't offer his cigarettes round/ when he is in company./ On cloudy days,/ she prefers to stay inside./ We had to work very hard yesterday/ and weren't very pleased about it,/ because it was a lovely, sunny day./ The car came round the bend/ in the road/ at top speed./ The driver was able/ to avoid the bike/ that was coming the other way,/ but went straight into the gate/ on the other side.

LESSON 66

344 **Past continuous** — **I was speaking**

particular — **while**

We use the present continuous for an action that is in progress now. For example, "I am speaking English now".

We use the past continuous for an action that was in progress at a particular time in the past. For example, "I was speaking English at this time yesterday". If I say "I was sleeping at 4 o'clock this morning", it means that I went to sleep before 4 o'clock and I woke up after 4 o'clock; at 4 o'clock, I was in the middle of a period of sleeping.

When do we use the present continuous? — We use the present continuous for an action that is in progress now

Give me an example, please. — I am speaking English now

When do we use the past continuous? — We use the past continuous for an action that was in progress at a particular time in the past

Give me an example, please. — I was speaking English at this time yesterday

The most common use of the past continuous is to say that an action was in progress when another action happened. For example, "I was cooking lunch when she arrived" means that, when she arrived, I was in the middle of cooking lunch.

Were you chatting to anybody when I came into the room at the beginning of the lesson? — Yes, I was ... when you ... ~ No, I wasn't ... when you ...

345 Were the students standing or sitting when I left the classroom at the end of the last lesson? — The students were ... when you left the classroom ...

Was it raining while you were coming to school today? Yes, it was raining while I was coming ... ~ No, it wasn't raining while I was coming ...

What were you doing at this time last Sunday? I was ... at this time last Sunday

Do you think most people in this town were sleeping at midnight last night? Yes, I think ...

Where were you living ten years ago? I was living ... ten years ago

earn

About how much does a doctor earn a year in your country? A doctor earns about ... a year in my country

formal informal jeans trainer

how do you do?

Would it be OK for a man to wear jeans and trainers if he was going to a formal dinner? No, it wouldn't be ...; he should wear a suit and tie

When we meet somebody for the first time, what can we say? When we meet ..., we can say "Nice to meet you"

And what do we say if we want to be more formal? If we want ..., we say "How do you do?"

And what does the other person reply? The other person replies "How do you do?"

346 persuade

Is it easy to persuade people to give their money away? No, it isn't easy ...; it's difficult

hairdresser

How often do you go to the hairdresser's? I go to the hairdresser's ... times a year

so **interesting** **exciting**

Why do you think some films are so popular? — I think ... because they tell interesting or exciting stories

grammatically

Is it grammatically correct to say "I've seen her yesterday"? — No, it isn't ...; we should say "I saw her yesterday" instead

bathroom **bath** **shower**

toilet **basin**

What does a bathroom usually contain? — A bathroom usually contains a bath or shower, a toilet and a basin

Which do you prefer: baths or showers? — I prefer ...

What's a rain shower? — A rain shower is a short period of rain

347 **mirror** **reflect**

What does a mirror do? — A mirror reflects light

In which rooms in a house do we usually find a mirror? — We usually find a mirror in a bathroom or a bedroom

Active and passive voice

active **passive**

subject **object**

Active voice

John broke the window

In the sentence "John broke the window", "John" is the subject and "the window" is the object. The verb, "broke", is in the active voice. All the verbs we have practised up to now have been in the active voice. The

active voice communicates that the subject is active and it does the action in the sentence.

Passive voice

The window was broken by John

This sentence, "The window was broken by John", has the same meaning, but the subject is now "The window", and the verb, "was broken", is in the passive voice. The passive voice communicates that the subject is passive; it does not do the action; it receives it.

348 **"To be" + past participle by**

We form the passive voice with the verb "to be" and a past participle. The verb "to be" communicates the time, and the past participle says what the action is. We use the word "by" when we want to say who does the action.

In the sentence "The window was broken by John", the word "was" tells us that the action happened in the past, the word "broken" tells us the action, and the words "by John" tell us who did the action.

What does the active voice communicate? — The active voice communicates that the subject does the action

What does the passive voice communicate? — The passive voice communicates that the subject receives the action

How do we form the passive voice? — We form the passive voice with the verb "to be" and a past participle

Give me some examples, please. — My car was washed last month. Many computers are made in China. The students will be taught by the teacher.

We must remember to put the verb "to be" in the right form. For example, "John has eaten pasta" becomes "Pasta has been eaten by John".

Now I am going to give you a sentence in the active voice, and I want you to put it into the passive voice:

John eats the pasta — The pasta is eaten by John

John ate the pasta	The pasta was eaten by John
John has eaten the pasta	The pasta has been eaten by John
349 **John will eat the pasta**	The pasta will be eaten by John
John is eating the pasta	The pasta is being eaten by John
John was eating the pasta	The pasta was being eaten by John
John would eat the pasta	The pasta would be eaten by John

Now we're going to practise with some different sentences:

I clean my car every Saturday	My car is cleaned by me every Saturday
She forgot him	He was forgotten by her
My boss is going to write that email	That email is going to be written by my boss
We are fixing the car	The car is being fixed by us
They have followed all the advice	All the advice has been followed by them

Dictation 40

They could perhaps meet/ a friend of theirs/ on their way home/ after the lesson./ He had a bad cold,/ but he refused/ to take any medicine./ You can learn words and grammar/ by reading books/ or using the internet./ However, you cannot learn/ how to speak a language well/ without practising it./ We must, therefore,/ try to speak/ as often as possible./ Do you have enough time/ to finish the work?

Do Revision Exercise 26

LESSON 67

350 **force** **make somebody do ...**

Do I force you to give long answers during the lesson?
Yes, you force me/us to give ...

Why? Because it is important to speak as much as possible

In the construction "make somebody do ...", the word "make" means "force" or "cause". For example, "The teacher made me correct my dictation" means that he forced me to correct my dictation. The sentence "Sunny weather makes me feel happy" means that it causes me to feel happy.

When you were a child, did your parents make you eat your vegetables?
Yes, when I was a child, my parents ...
~ No, when I was a child, my parents didn't ...

What kind of films make you laugh? The kind of films that make me laugh are ...

snack **break** **biscuit** **crisps**

What is a snack? A snack is something small that people eat between meals, like a sandwich or a bag of crisps

Which would you prefer as a snack during a morning break: a bag of crisps or some biscuits?
I'd prefer ...

to be born

Where were you born? I was born in ...

351 How soon after you were born did you learn to walk? I learnt to walk about a year after I was born

murder

Do you like reading books with stories about murders in them?
Yes, I like ... ~ No, I don't like ...

prison

Would you like to see inside a prison?

Yes, I'd like ... ~ No, I wouldn't like ...

Why or why not?

Because I'd find it interesting ~ Because it'd make me feel very unhappy

pupil

What's a pupil?

A pupil is a child who's in school

Do most pupils in your country have to wear a uniform?

Yes, most pupils in my country ... ~ No, most pupils in my country don't ...

root

What do we call the part of a tree that's in the land?

We call the part ... the roots

memory

Have you got a good memory?

Yes, I've got ... ~ No, I haven't got ...

352 **Another contraction of the verb "to be"**

I'm	not	I'm	not
you	aren't	you're	not
he	isn't	he's	not
she	isn't	she's	not
it	isn't	it's	not
we	aren't	we're	not
you	aren't	you're	not
they	aren't	they're	not

Instead of "I'm not", "you aren't", "he isn't" etc., we can use "I'm not", "you're not", "he's not" etc.

What can we use instead of "I'm not", "you aren't", "he isn't" etc.?
Instead of "I'm not", "you aren't", "he isn't" etc., we can use "I'm not", "you're not", "he's not", "she's not", "it's not", "we're not", "you're not", "they're not"

cross

If you want to go from one side of the road to the other, what must you do?
If I want ..., I must cross the road

What must you do before crossing the road?
I must look both ways before ...

353 If you wanted to go from here to Scotland, would you have to cross the sea or would you be able to go all the way by land?
If I wanted ..., I'd ...

think of

What was the first thing you thought of when you woke up this morning?
The first thing I thought of when I ... was ...

safe   safety   on your own

What's the opposite of the word "dangerous"?
The opposite ... is "safe"

Do you think it's safe to shop online?
Yes, I think ... ~ No, I don't think ...

Do parents often worry about their children's safety?
Yes, parents often ...

Is it safe for young children to cross the road on their own?
No, it isn't ...

Do you like going on holiday on your own?
Yes, I like ... on my own ~ No, I don't like ... on my own; I prefer going in company

lay

What's the past of the verb "to lie"?
The past of ... is "lay"

How long did you lie in bed for last night?
I lay in bed for ... hours last night

354 **sir** **madam** **gentleman** **lady**

customer **officer**

To be polite, people who work in shops, hotels etc. use the words "sir", "madam" or "miss" when they speak to customers. Also, in the army, a soldier calls his officer "sir", and at school, a pupil sometimes calls his teacher "sir" or "miss".

When do people use the words "sir" and "madam"?

People use ... to be polite when they are speaking to their customers in a shop, their officers in the army, or their teachers at school

Give me an example, please.

"Excuse me sir; can I help you?"

When we want to sound polite, we can use the words "gentleman" and "lady" instead of "man" and "woman". For example, we can say "Who is that gentleman over there?" or "The lady I spoke to on the phone yesterday told me to call again today".

When do we use the words "gentleman" and "lady"?

We use ... instead of "man" and "woman" when we want to sound polite

Give me an example, please.

"Which of these two gentlemen gave you the book?" and "Will you ask that lady her name, please?"

title

Everybody has a title. For most people, it is "Mr", "Mrs", "Miss" or "Ms". For example, John Brown's title is "Mr", so we call him "Mr Brown". The title "Mrs" is for married women; the title "Miss" is for unmarried women; the title "Ms" can be used for either married or unmarried women.

355 **Some people have other titles, such as "Sir" and "Lady". For example "Sir Paul McCartney" and "Lady Diana".**

What's your title?

My title is "..."

Give me examples of "Sir" and "Lady" used as titles.

Some examples ... are "Sir Paul McCartney" and "Lady Diana"

standard height

Which two countries have the highest standards of living in the world?

... and ... have the highest standards of living in the world

What's the standard height for a man (or woman) in this country?

The standard height ... is ...

colourful

Dictation 41

Sixteenth century fashions/ in men's clothes/ were very colourful./ The word "use" is a verb,/ whilst the word "use" is a noun./ After the verb "succeed",/ we use the word "in"/ followed by a gerund./ For example,/ "He succeeded in answering the question."/ He is only a beginner,/ but believes he will succeed./ I hope so./ A hard worker/ rarely fails an examination,/ so students should always work hard.

LESSON 68

356 **would you say** **opinion**

We use the expression "would you say" when we ask somebody for his opinion about something. It means "Do you think ... ?"

When do we use the expression "would you say"? We use the expression ...

Would you say that a king's life was better than that of the average man? Yes, I'd say ... ~ No, I wouldn't say ...

Notice that we use the past tense after "would you say", because it is part of a conditional construction.

Which tense do we use after the expression "would you say"? We use the past tense after ...

What would you say was the best way to remember something? I'd say that the best ... was to repeat it often

"Look" + adjective

If the sky looks dark and cloudy, do you sometimes decide not to go out? Yes, if the sky ..., I sometimes ...

When your shoes look dirty, what do you do? When my shoes ..., I clean them

357 **get in** **get out of**

get on **get off** **taxi** **fare**

We get in/into a car, but we get on/onto a bus, a train, a plane or a ship.
We get out of a car, but we get off a bus, a train, a plane or a ship.

Do we pay the driver when we get in a taxi? No, we don't ...; we pay when we get out of a taxi

In your country, do you have to buy a ticket before getting on a bus?

Yes, in my country, you have to ... ~ No, in my country, you don't have to ...; you can just pay when you get on

How much is the bus fare from here to where you live?

The bus fare ... where I live is ...

royal

Has your country got a royal family?

Yes, my country's got ... ~ No, my country hasn't got ...

mud **countryside**

How do we get mud on our shoes?

We get mud ... by walking in the countryside in the rain

crowd **crowded**

Are famous actors often surrounded by crowds when they go out in public?

Yes, famous actors are ...

Are the buses in this town usually crowded in the morning?

Yes, the buses ... ~ No, the buses ...

358 **captain** **team**

Have you ever been the captain of a sports team?

Yes, I've been ... ~ No, I've never been ...

Tell me the name of a famous sea captain.

The name of ... is Captain Cook/Nemo etc.

wide **narrow**

Which is the widest street in the place where you live, and which is the narrowest?

... is the widest street in ..., and ... is the narrowest

flag **national**

What colour is the flag of your country?

The flag of my country is ...

Do you know the origin of your national flag?

Yes, I know ... ~ No, I don't know ...

grass **live on**

If we say "John lives on pasta", we mean that John only eats pasta.

Name an animal that lives on grass. A horse is an animal ...

What happens to grass if there's no rain? If there's no rain, grass becomes yellow and then it dies

359 **tower**

Where is the nearest tower to the place where you live? The nearest tower ... I live is ...

wet **dry**

Are the streets dry when it rains? No, the streets aren't ...; they're wet

If you walked in the rain without an umbrella, what'd happen? If I walked ..., I'd get wet

If you got wet, what'd you have to do with your clothes? If I got wet, I'd have to take my clothes off and hang them up to dry

threw

What's the past of "throw"? The past of "throw" is "threw"

What'd happen if I threw a stone at the window? If you threw ..., the window'd break

loud **turn up** **turn down**

If your TV is turned up too loud, what do you do? If my TV ..., I turn it down

360 **Reflexive pronouns**

myself	**yourself**	**himself**
herself	**itself**	**oneself**

ourselves **yourselves** **themselves**

consequently **protect**

We use a reflexive pronoun when the subject and object are the same person or thing. In the sentence "The teacher taught me", the subject and the object are different people. In the sentence "I taught myself", the subject and the object are the same person. Consequently, we use the reflexive pronoun "myself" as the object.

What are the reflexive pronouns? — The reflexive pronouns are "myself", "yourself", "himself", "herself", "itself", "oneself", "ourselves", "yourselves" and "themselves"

When do we use a reflexive pronoun? — We use a reflexive pronoun when the subject and object are the same person or thing

Is it right to say "I looked at me in the mirror"? — No, it isn't right ...

Why not? — Because the subject and object are the same person

What must we say instead? — We must say "I looked at myself in the mirror" instead

Do you think it'd be easy for me to teach myself Chinese (Arabic etc.)? — No, I don't think ... for you to teach yourself ...

Why not? — Because ... is a difficult language to learn

361 Did you wash yourself when you were a baby? — No, I didn't wash myself when I was a baby; my mother washed me

What'd you do if you saw a man trying to kill himself? — If I saw ..., I'd try to stop him or call the police

Have you ever seen a bird washing itself? — Yes, I've seen ... ~ No, I've never seen ...

Do you think one can teach oneself a language? — Yes, I think ... ~ No, I don't think ...

What do we carry to protect ourselves from the rain? — We carry an umbrella to protect ...

Do Revision Exercise 27

LESSON 69

362 **thorough** (completo) **thorougly** (completamente)

What does the word "thorough" mean? The word "thorough" means "complete"

In which season of the year do people generally give their houses a thorough cleaning? People generally ... in spring

If you jumped into the sea, would you get thoroughly wet? Yes, if I ..., I'd get ...

What kind of things make you thoroughly tired? The kind of things that make me thoroughly tired are hard physical work, studying a lot without a break, not enough sleep etc.

accident **by accident**

If you drove a car on the left-hand side of the road (in America, France etc.) instead of on the right, what'd happen? If I drove ..., I'd have an accident

Have you ever seen an accident on the road? Yes, I've seen ... ~ No, I've never seen ...

If you took something by accident that didn't belong to you, what'd you do? If I took ... to me, I'd return it

363 **careful** **careless** **carefully** **carelessly**

Do people become careless when they're in great danger? No, people don't ...; they become very careful

Do you write carefully? Yes, I write ... ~ No, I don't ...; I write carelessly

What could happen if you were careless when crossing the road? If I were ..., I could have an accident

Of all the people you know, who dresses the most carelessly? Of all the people I know, ... dresses the most carelessly

own (poseer)

Do you own all the clothes you're wearing, or do any of them belong to somebody else?
I own ... I'm wearing ~ I don't own ... I'm wearing; some of them belong to somebody else

What would you like to own more than anything else?
I'd like to own ... more than anything else

Who owns the place where you live?
... own(s) the place where I live ~ I don't know who owns the place where I live

carry on (seguir, continuar) retire (jubilarse)

Do people in your country usually carry on working after they reach the age of 65?
Yes, people in my country ... ~ No, people in my country ...; they retire

364 prize (premio)

Have you ever won a prize for anything?
Yes, I've won a prize for something ~ No, I've never won a prize for anything

What?

too (también)

Give me a sentence with the word "too", meaning "also".
He wants a biscuit, and I want one too

at least (al menos, por lo menos)

Give me a sentence with the words "at least" in it.
I've asked him at least six times, and each time he has forgotten ~ He didn't do very well in the exam, but at least he passed

widely (ampliamente)

Which is one of the most widely used English adjectives?
One of the ... is "nice" ("good" etc.)

Is English the most widely spoken language in the world? Yes, English is ...

manner **pig**

Why are good manners so important in life? Good manners are ... because they make life easier and more pleasant

365 What do we mean when we say that somebody has the manners of a pig? When we say ..., we mean that they have very bad manners

Do people in very hot countries dress in the same manner as people in very cold countries? No, people in ...; they dress in a different manner

asleep **awake**

Will you still be asleep at 11 o'clock tomorrow morning? No, I won't still be ...; I'll be awake

Will you still be awake at 3 o'clock tomorrow morning? No, I won't still be ...; I'll be asleep

hospital **nurse**

Who takes care of us when we're in hospital? Nurses and doctors take ...

purpose **in order to ...** **so that**

take exercise

The most common way to communicate purpose in English is by using the infinitive with "to". For example, the sentence "I went to the hospital to see a doctor" tells us the purpose of going to the hospital. With formal English, it is more common to use "in order to". For example, we would say "I visited the hospital in order to see a doctor".

366 Answer the following questions with "in order to":

Why do people eat? — People eat in order to live

For what purpose do people work? — People work in order to earn money

What must we do in order to keep in good health? — In order to ..., we must sleep well, eat healthy food, take plenty of exercise, not smoke etc.

What do you think is the purpose of living? — I think the ... is to be happy and to make others happy etc.

We can also use "so that" to communicate purpose. For example, "She shut the door so that the cat could not go into the garden".

Give me an example of "so that", please. — He put the food in the fridge so that it would stay fresh

notice (

Are there any notices hanging up in the school? — Yes, there are some ... ~ No, there aren't any ...

Where?

What do they say?

lain (tumbarse)

What are the three forms of "lie"? — The three forms of "lie" are "lie, lay, lain"

What's the longest you've ever lain in bed for when you've been ill? — The longest I've ever ... when I've been ill is about ...

367 **point at** (señalar dedo) **point out** (destacar) **indicate** (indicar)

We use "point at" for the action of pointing the finger at an object. For example, "I'm pointing at that picture". However, "to point out" means to indicate something among different things. For example, "He pointed out the mistakes in my dictation".

What's the difference between "to point at" and "to point out"?

The difference between "to point at" and "to point out" is that we use "to point at" for the action of pointing the finger at an object, whereas "to point out" means to indicate something among different things

What am I doing?

You're pointing at the light

Point at the picture on the wall, please.

What are you doing?

I'm pointing at ...

Point out the mistake in this sentence, please: "I've gone to the cinema this week".

We can't say "I've gone ..."; we must say "I've been to the cinema this week"

What's he doing?

He's pointing out the mistake in that sentence

grave

In your country, do people visit their relatives' graves?

Yes, in my country, people ...
~ No, in my country, people ...

368 neck

Is it bad for your neck to sleep without a pillow?

Yes, it's bad ...
~ No, it isn't bad ...

flame

Can we have a fire without flames?

Yes, we can ...

flight

How long is the flight from here to …?

The flight from ...

soup (sopa) **except**

Dictation 42 26/10/18

The flag on top of the tower/ is wide at one end/ and narrow at the other./ Thin soup is very pleasant,/ but I prefer a big bowl/ of thick soup/ when I'm hungry./ Except for me,/ nobody knew that our actions/ were against the law./ He gets angry/ when he loses his way/ and has to ask a policeman./ I'll continue swimming/ until I feel tired./ Fish can't stay alive/ without water.

LESSON 70

369 **may** **might** **palace**

parliament

The words "may" and "might" both express the idea of "perhaps", but we cannot use "may" in the 2nd conditional. For example, we cannot say "If I was rich, I may buy a big house "; we must say "I might buy" instead.

What do the words "may" and "might" express? — The words "may" and "might" express the idea of "perhaps"

What's the difference between "may" and "might"? — The difference between "may" and "might" is that we cannot use "may" in the 2nd conditional

Give me an example. — If I went to London, I might visit Buckingham Palace

Do you think it may rain later? — Yes, I think it may rain later ~ No, I don't think it will rain later

What do you think I might have in my pocket? — I think you might have ... in your pocket

What might happen if you didn't look both ways before crossing the road? — An accident might happen if I didn't ...

What might you see if you went to London? — I might see Buckingham Palace, the Houses of Parliament, Trafalgar Square, Piccadilly Circus etc. if I went to London

Do you think there might be another world war? — Yes, I think there might be ... ~ No, I don't think there'll be ...

370 **arrive at** **point** **arrive in** **area**

airport **passport**

We arrive at a point, like a building or a station, whereas we arrive in an area, like a city or a country.

What's the difference between "arrive at" and "arrive in"?

The difference between "arrive at" and "arrive in" is that we arrive at a point, whereas we arrive in an area

What time do you arrive at school?

I arrive at school at ...

If you arrived at a foreign airport without your passport, what might happen?

If I arrived ... without my passport, I might not be able to enter the country

café (cafeteria)

What is a café?

A café is a small, informal restaurant where you can get light meals, snacks and drinks

owe (deber: Dinero o explicación)

Do you owe me any money?

Yes, I owe you some money
~ No, I don't owe you any money

Do I owe you any money?

Yes, you owe me some money
~ No, you don't owe me any money

Verb + back

souvenir (recuerdo)

When we add the word "back" to a verb it means "to return". For example, "give back", "go back", "pay back" etc.

371 **What does it mean "to give back"?**

"To give back" means "to return"

When you go on holiday, what do you bring back with you?

When I go ..., I bring back souvenirs with me

Are you going to go back home immediately after the lesson's ended?

Yes, I'm going to go ...
~ No, I'm not going to go ...

When people lend you money, do you always pay it back when promised?

Yes, when people lend me money, I always ...
~ No, when people lend me money, I don't always ...

Do you know anybody who has retired but then later gone back to work?

Yes, I know somebody ...
~ No, I don't know anybody ...

pride **proud** **normal** **normally**

take pride in

What is your normal breakfast? My normal breakfast is ...

Do people normally feel proud when they do well in exams? Yes, people normally ...

Do you take pride in your work (studies)? Yes, I take pride in my work (studies) ~ No I don't take pride in my work (studies)

servant

If you were very rich, would you have servants in your house? Yes, if I were ..., I'd have servants in my house ~ No, if I were ..., I wouldn't have servants in my house

372 **wheel** **lorry**

Does a lorry have fewer wheels than a car? No, a lorry doesn't ...; it has more wheels

arrow **centimetre** **metre**

About how long is an arrow? An arrow is about a metre long

How many centimetres make a metre? A hundred centimetres make a metre

beard

Do you know anybody who has a long beard? Yes, I know somebody ... ~ No I don't know anybody ...

true **false** **paper (newspaper)**

Is it false that the opposite of "heaven" is "hell"? No, it isn't false ...; it's true

Is everything we read in the newspapers true? No, not everything ...; some things are true and some things are false

Why do you think this is so?

I think maybe it's because newspapers haven't always got time to make sure that what they write is completely true

maintain

Is it cheap to maintain a large house?

No, it isn't cheap ...; it's expensive

373 **it takes** **Ireland**

How do we translate the words "it takes"?

We translate ... with "..."

How long does it take you to go home from here?

It takes me about ... to go ...

Does it take longer to fly from here to Ireland than to go by train and ship?

No, it doesn't take ...; it takes less time

About how long would it take us to reach the station from here if we walked very fast?

It'd take us about ... to reach ...

amount **amount to**

What amount of money have you got in your pocket (or bag) at the moment?

I've got about ... in my pocket ...

Do they use a large amount of wood in building houses in this region?

Yes, they use ... ~ No, they don't use ...

Why or why not?

Because it's cheap/expensive etc.

What do £50 and £13 amount to?

£50 and £13 amount to £63

further **Sweden** **in addition**

extra

The word "further" means the same as "farther", but it also means "in addition" or "extra".

What does the word "further" mean?

The word "further" ...

374 **Which is further from Spain: Sweden or Switzerland?**

Sweden is further from Spain than Switzerland

What's the furthest you've ever been?

The furthest I've ever been is from ... to ...

Where'd you have to go if you wanted further information about train times at a station?

I'd have to go to the information office if I wanted ...

Give me a further example of the word "further", please.

If I failed an exam, I'd have to take further lessons

Dictation 43

They keep lots of their books/ under the bed./ She's pouring the fruit juice/ from a bottle into a glass./ His grave/ was covered with sand,/ and, in the sand,/ somebody had printed his name./ From the neck of the bottle/ came a flame/ which gave light to the room./ Fish and chips/ is a common meal in England./ If we push a door/ which has the word "pull"/ written on it,/ it won't open./ He's got a hole in his sock.

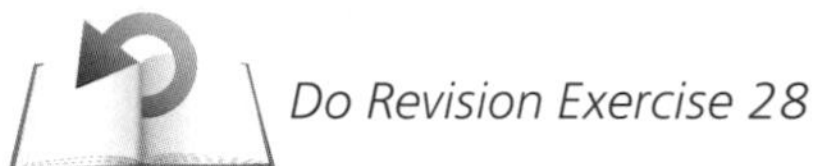

Do Revision Exercise 28

LESSON 71

375 **Past perfect** **I had eaten**

The past perfect communicates the same idea as the present perfect except that, instead of thinking about time before and up to now, we are thinking about time before and up to a specific point in the past. For example, with the present perfect, we can say "Mary cannot enter her flat because she has lost her key". With the past perfect, we can say "Mary could not enter her flat yesterday because she had lost her key".

When do we use the present perfect?

We use the present perfect when we are thinking about time before and up to now

Give me an example.

Mary cannot enter her flat because she has lost her key

What does that sentence mean?

That sentence means that Mary does not know where her key is now because of losing it earlier today

When do we use the past perfect?

We use the past perfect when we are thinking about time before and up to another point in the past

Give me an example.

Mary could not enter her flat yesterday because she had lost her key

What does that sentence mean?

That sentence means that Mary did not know where her key was yesterday because of losing it earlier in the day

376 What's the difference between these two sentences?

"I ate my dinner at 9 o'clock"

and

"I had eaten my dinner at 9 o'clock"

The difference between these two sentences is that "I ate my dinner at 9 o'clock" means I started to eat my dinner at 9 o'clock, whereas "I had eaten my dinner at 9 o'clock" means that my dinner was already finished at 9 o'clock

Had you had anything to eat before you came to school today?

Yes, I had had something ... before I came ...
~ No, I hadn't had anything ... before I came ...

Had you ever seen me before you came to this school?

Yes, I had seen you before I came ...
~ No, I had never seen you before I came ...

When you began your lessons at this school, had you already studied some English or were you a complete beginner?

When I began my lessons ..., I had already ...
~ When I began my lessons ..., I hadn't studied any English; I was a complete beginner

party political

What does the word "party" mean?

The word "party" means ...

Do you ever throw (have) a party at home on your birthday?

Yes, I sometimes ... on my birthday ~ No, I never ... on my birthday

Which is the strongest political party in your country today?

The ... party is the ... in my country today

Do you prefer to go on holiday with a friend or in a large party?

I prefer to go on ...

377 mad crazy UFO

The word "mad" has three common meanings: angry, very interested, and crazy.

What does the word "mad" mean?

The word "mad" means angry, very interested, and crazy

Do some people get mad when they're driving in very heavy traffic?

Yes, some people ...

What kind of things are you most mad about?

I'm most mad about music, films, sport etc.

If a friend told you they had seen a UFO, would you believe them or think they were going mad?

If a friend told me ..., I'd ...

copy

What happens if one pupil copies from another during an exam?

If one pupil ..., he's sent out of the room

When you answer a question during a Callan lesson, should you simply copy what the teacher says?

No, when I answer ..., I shouldn't simply ...; I should try to answer the question without waiting to hear the words from the teacher first

If you were given two copies of the same book for your birthday, what would you do?

If I were given ... for my birthday, I'd ...

378 influence

Does the weather have a strong influence over you? Do you, for example, feel happy in good weather and unhappy in bad weather?

Yes, the weather ... over me
~ No, the weather ... over me

mouse mice

What is the name of the famous mouse in the cinema world?

The name of ... is Mickey Mouse

What do mice like eating?

Mice like eating cheese etc.

throat

What part of the body's this?

It's the throat

opportunity

Which would you prefer: a job that gave you the opportunity to visit other countries, or a job that gave you the opportunity to earn a lot?

I'd prefer a job that gave me the opportunity to ...

develop industry agriculture

What do we mean by the under-developed countries of the world?

By the under-developed ..., we mean those with little industry, agriculture etc.

379 **print**

Where was this book printed?

This book was printed in ...

sand beach desert

Where do we find sand?

We find sand on a beach, in a desert etc.

When you're on holiday, do you enjoy lying on a beach in the sun?

Yes, when I'm ..., I enjoy ...
~ No, when I'm ..., I don't enjoy ...

Why is it difficult to live in a desert?

It's difficult ... because there is so little water

bell knock pay a visit ring

What am I doing?

You're knocking on the table

Is there a bell in this school?

Yes, there's a bell ...
~ No, there isn't a bell ...

What do you do when you arrive at somebody's front door in order to pay a visit?

When I arrive at ..., I knock on the door or ring the doorbell

shout

When do people shout?

People shout when they're angry or when they think somebody can't hear them

If there were some people shouting loudly outside in the corridor, would you be able to hear me?

No, if there were ..., I wouldn't be able to hear you

stick — walking stick

Do some people use walking sticks to help them move around when they get older? Yes, some people ...

Which animals like to fetch sticks that you throw for them? Dogs like to fetch ...

Would prefer + infinitive with "to"

Where would you prefer to live: by a lake or by the sea? I'd prefer to live by ...

This evening, would you prefer to go out for dinner or simply go home? This evening, I'd prefer to ...

exclamation mark

Dictation 44

Keep off the grass!/ They've gone away for the day/ and will return late/ this evening;/ at least, that's what they said/ before leaving./ The average age/ for getting married/ is between twenty and thirty./ Among all the subjects/ I studied at school,/ I found science/ the most interesting,/ not the most boring./ Birds cannot fly/ faster than planes./ The soldiers carried the sticks/ into the field/ in order to make a fire.

LESSON 72

381 **-ness** **reason**

illness **tiredness** **darkness**

To form a noun from an adjective, we sometimes add the letters "ness" to the adjective. For example, "slow – slowness", "late – lateness", "careless – carelessness" etc.

How do we sometimes form a noun from an adjective? — We sometimes form a noun from an adjective by adding the letters "ness" to the adjective

Give me an example. — late – lateness

When did you have your last illness? — I had my last illness ...

What's the reason for tiredness? — The reason for tiredness is too much work, not enough sleep etc.

What's the reason for darkness at night? — The reason for darkness at night is that the world turns completely round every 24 hours

alone

What's another way of saying "he lives on his own"? — Another way ... is "He lives alone"

Do you live alone or with other people? — I live alone ~ I live with other people

Do you prefer to go on holiday alone? — Yes, I prefer ... ~ No, I don't prefer ...; I prefer to go in company

382 **already**

Has the lesson already finished? — No, the lesson hasn't finished yet; it's still in progress

Are you already able to speak English without making any mistakes? — No, I'm not able to ... yet; I still make some mistakes

Are we already in spring (summer etc.)? No, we aren't in ... yet; we're still in ...

Have we already studied Stage 4 of the Callan Method? Yes, we've already studied ...

thrown

What are the three forms of "throw"? The three forms of "throw" are "throw, threw, thrown"

Have you ever thrown anything away by mistake which was worth a lot of money? Yes, I've thrown something away ... ~ No, I've never thrown anything away ...

What?

in spite of despite

"In spite of" and "despite" both mean the same as "although", but they are prepositions, so we put nouns after them.

There are three ways of using "in spite of" or "despite". They can be followed by a noun, or "-ing", or "the fact that ...". For example:

In spite of her illness, she went to work.

Despite being ill, she went to work.

In spite of the fact that she was ill, she went to work.

383 **It is important to remember that "in spite of" and "despite" cannot be followed immediately by a subject and verb. For example, we <u>cannot</u> say "In spite of she was ill, she went to work".**

Why do some people do dangerous sports in spite of the danger? Some people ... because they find them exciting

Name some foods that are very popular despite being bad for the health. Some foods that are very ... are ...

Do you think it's worth learning a foreign language in spite of the fact that it's quite difficult? Yes, I think ...

In spite of studying a lot of words and grammar, do you still find English a little difficult? Yes, in spite of ..., I still find ...

anyone someone no one (no–one)

Instead of the words "anybody", "somebody" and "nobody", we can use the words "anyone", "someone" and "no one" (or "no-one").

What words can we use instead of "anybody", "somebody" and "nobody"?
Instead of "anybody", "somebody" and "nobody", we can use "anyone", "someone" and "no one"

Did anyone come into the classroom at the beginning of the lesson?
Yes, someone came ...

Who went out of this room two minutes ago?
No one went ...

384 borrow

What's the opposite of the verb "to lend"?
The opposite ... is "to borrow"

Should we always give back the things we borrow?
Yes, we should always ...

If you forgot to bring a pen with you to school, would you have to borrow one from another student?
Yes, if I forgot ... with me to school, I'd have to ...

my own emphasize

We often put the word "own" after a possessive adjective when we want to emphasize that something belongs to someone. For example, this is my own pen; it belongs to me. Notice that we can say that this is our classroom because we study here all the time, but we cannot say that this is our own classroom because it doesn't belong to us.

Give me an example of the word "own" after a possessive adjective.
This is my own book

Do you live in your own house (or flat), or does it belong to somebody else?
Yes, I live in my own house (or flat) ~ No, I don't live in my own house (or flat); it belongs to ...

Do you think this is probably my own book or do you think it belongs to the school?
I think that's probably your own book ~ I don't think that's your own book; I think it belongs ...

skin

What's this? — It's your skin

385 **wire** **electricity**

connection **wireless** **Wi–Fi**

hyphen

What do we use wire for? — We use wire to carry electricity, to connect things together etc.

What do we mean by a wireless internet connection? — By a wireless internet connection, we mean that we can connect to the internet without connecting wires to our computer

What can we say instead of "a wireless internet connection"? — Instead of ..., we can say "Wi-Fi"

Do some bars and cafés offer free Wi-Fi to their customers? — Yes, some bars ...

Spell the word "Wi-Fi", please. — W, I, hyphen, F, I

boil **fry** **roast**

Tell me three ways of cooking potatoes. — Three ways ... are boiling, frying and roasting

Do you prefer fried eggs or boiled eggs? — I prefer ...

How long does it take to boil potatoes? — It takes about twenty minutes to boil potatoes

brick

What's a wall normally built of? — A wall is normally built of bricks

as well too also

The words "as well", "too" and "also" all mean the same thing. The words "as well" and "too" go at the end of the sentence, but the word "also" usually goes after the first auxiliary verb.

Where do the words "as well", "too" and "also" usually go?

The words "as well" and "too" go at the end of the sentence, but the word "also" usually goes after the first auxiliary verb.

Give me an example of each, please.

I will be sleeping at 3 a.m.; my sister will be sleeping as well; my mother will be sleeping too; my brother will also be sleeping.

With the present simple and past simple, there is no auxiliary in the positive, so the word "also" simply goes between the subject and the verb. For example, we say "He speaks German and he also speaks French".

Give me an example of "also" when there is no auxiliary verb, please.

I love coffee and I also love tea

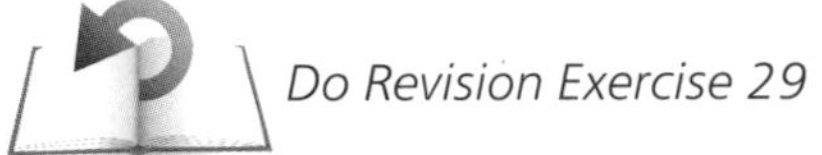
Do Revision Exercise 29

LESSON 73

387 **Future continuous** **I will be speaking**

We use the future continuous for an action that will be in progress at a particular time in the future. For example, the sentence "I will be sleeping at 4 o'clock tomorrow morning" means that I will go to sleep before 4 o'clock and I will wake up after 4 o'clock; at 4 o'clock, I will be in the middle of a period of sleeping.

When do we use the future continuous? — We use the future continuous ...

Give me an example, please. — I will be working at this time tomorrow

What do you think you will be doing at this time tomorrow? — I think I'll be ... at this time tomorrow

Will you still be studying English in fifty years' time? — No, I won't still be studying ...

Where do you think you'll be living in ten years' time? — I think I'll be living ... in ten years' time

inch **foot** **yard**

This is an inch; this is a foot; this is a yard. An inch is about two-and-a-half centimetres. Twelve inches make a foot, and three feet make a yard. A yard is about three inches shorter than a metre.

What's this? — It's an inch

388 What's this? — It's a foot

What's this? — It's a yard

How many centimetres make an inch? — About two and a half centimetres make an inch

How many inches make a foot? — Twelve inches make a foot

How many feet make a yard? — Three feet make a yard

Is a yard longer than a metre? No, a yard ...; it's shorter than a metre

Consequently, when we run a hundred yards, do we run further than a hundred metres? No, when we run ...; we run less than ...

chain

Are you wearing a chain? Yes, I'm ... ~ No, I'm not ...

What do we mean when we say someone is a chain-smoker? When we say ..., we mean that he or she smokes one cigarette after another without stopping, like a chain

rise constantly

What's my book doing? Your book's rising in the air

Does the sun rise early in winter? No, the sun doesn't ...; it rises late

Is the cost of living constantly rising these days? Yes, the cost of living is ... ~ No, the cost of living isn't ...

389 What'd you do if this table slowly began to rise into the air without anybody touching it? If this table ..., I'd run out of the room etc.

belt

Are you wearing a belt? Yes, I'm ... ~ No, I'm not ...

hourly daily weekly monthly yearly

The words "hourly", "daily", "weekly", "monthly" and "yearly" mean "every hour", "every day", "every week", "every month" and "every year".

What do the words "hourly", "daily", "weekly", "monthly" and "yearly" mean? The words "hourly", "daily" ... mean "every hour", "every day" ...

Do most radio stations have hourly traffic news? Yes, most radio stations ...

Which daily newspaper do you read? I read ...

Do you read any weekly newspapers? Yes, I read some ... ~ No, I don't read any ...

Which?

How many hours of English do you study monthly? I study ... hours of English monthly

Where do you usually go for your yearly holidays? I usually go ... for my yearly holidays

390 **allow** **let – let – let** **everyday**

The verbs "allow" and "let" have the same meaning. The difference is that "allow" has the infinitive with "to" after it, whereas "let" has the infinitive without "to" after it. For example, we can say "The policeman allowed the man to go home" or "The policeman let the man go home". In everyday English, "let" is more common than "allow".

What's the difference between "allow" and "let"? The difference between "allow" and "let" is that "allow" has the infinitive with "to" after it, whereas "let" has the infinitive without "to" after it

Give me an example, please. The doctor allowed me to change my appointment. The doctor let me change my appointment.

What sometimes happens when we let people borrow things that belong to us? When we let ..., they sometimes don't return them

Do you think it's a good idea to allow children to do as they please (want to)? No, I don't think ...

Do you think it's dangerous these days to let people we don't know enter our houses? Yes, I think ... ~ No, I don't think ...

Do you think more people would kill each other if the law of the country let them? Yes, I think ... ~ No, I don't think ...

Another difference between "allow" and "let" is that we cannot use "let" in the passive voice. We cannot say "I was let"; we must say "I was allowed".

Which is it right to say: "I was let" or "I was allowed"? It's right to say "I was allowed"

Why? Because we cannot use "let" in the passive voice

Do you think students should be allowed to use their mobile phones during lessons? Yes, I think ... ~ No, I don't think ...

391  *Dictation 45*

From over the lake/ came the sound/ of the church bells. /The fat man swam/ better than his thin friend./ She lost her way/ and was unable to find a policeman./ Some past participles of verbs are:/ begun, known, swum,/ taken, shaken, written,/ forgotten and broken./ We use the word "whether"/ to express a doubt./ The only way to learn/ how to cook/ is by practice.

LESSON 74

392

Anywhere?	**somewhere** **not anywhere**
Where?	on the wall **nowhere**

Is there a book anywhere in this room? Yes, there's a book somewhere in this room

Is there a radio anywhere in this room? No, there isn't a radio anywhere in this room

If there's nowhere to sit on a bus, what do you have to do? If there's nowhere ..., I have to stand

Is there anywhere near here I can buy foreign books? Yes, there's somewhere near here you can ...

Is there anywhere in this town I could get my hair cut for nothing? No, there isn't ... you could get your hair cut for nothing

Where in the world can a man murder another man without breaking the law? There's nowhere in the world ...

If you could live anywhere in the world, where would you live? If I could live ..., I'd live in ...

Why?

393 **loose** **loosen**

Do you think it's OK to let dogs run around loose, or do you think they should be kept on a chain? I think it's OK ... ~ I think dogs should ...

Why do people in hot countries wear loose clothes? People in hot countries ... to keep themselves cool

Are there any loose stones on the road outside this school? Yes, there are some ... ~ No, there aren't any ...

Why does a man sometimes loosen his tie? — A man sometimes ... because it's more comfortable

storm lightning thunder

What's a storm? — A storm is a short period of very bad weather

What do we sometimes see and hear in a storm? — We sometimes see lightning and hear thunder in a storm

blind

How do blind people read? — Blind people read with special books made for them, which they can read by touching the words

devil

Where does the devil live? — The devil lives in hell

394 ride cycle

Can you ride a horse? — Yes, I can ... ~ No, I can't ...

Do you like riding on buses? — Yes, I like ... ~ No, I don't like ...

What's another way of saying "I ride a bike every day"? — Another way ... is "I cycle every day"

may can could permission

When we ask for permission to do something, we use the words "may", "can" or "could". For example, "May I leave the room, please?"

What words do we use when we ask for permission to do something? — We use "may", "can" or "could" when we ask ...

Give me three examples, please. — May I smoke? Can I open the window? Could I borrow your pen, please?

catch raincoat

We use the word "catch" in expressions such as "catch a ball", "catch a train", "catch a cold" etc.

In what kind of expressions do we use the word "catch"? We use the word "catch" in expressions such as ...

What am I doing? You're throwing your pen into the air and catching it

395 Are you the kind of person who usually has to run hard at the last moment in order to catch a bus or a train? Yes, I'm the kind of ... ~ No, I'm not the kind of ...

If you walked in the rain without carrying an umbrella or wearing a raincoat, what might happen? If I walked ..., I'd get wet and might catch a cold

cap

Why is it a good idea to wear a cap in hot, sunny weather? It's a good idea ... because it protects your head and eyes from the sun

habit — be in the habit of doing

The most common way to speak about our habits is to use the present simple or past simple. For example, we say "I drink coffee every day" or "I usually went to bed early when I was a child". We sometimes add expressions like "usually", "always" or "every week" so that it is understood that we are speaking about a habit.

What's the most common way to speak about our habits? The most common ...

Give me an example, please. I play football every weekend. I always studied hard before exams at university

Does your father smoke? Yes, my father smokes ~ No, my father doesn't smoke

Did you usually go to bed early when you were a small child? Yes, I usually went to bed early when I was ...

What's your worst habit? My worst habit is that I (smoke, drink too much coffee etc.)

Notice that we can also say that someone is "in the habit of doing" something.

396 Are you in the habit of speaking to yourself when you're alone?

Yes, I'm in the ... to myself when I'm alone
~ No, I'm not in the ... to myself when I'm alone

What were you in the habit of doing at the weekend when you were a little child?

I was in the habit of ... at the weekend when I was ...

stranger foreigner

A stranger is somebody we don't know, whereas a foreigner is somebody from another country.

What's the difference between a stranger and a foreigner?

The difference between a stranger and a foreigner is that a stranger is ...

snowstorm

Dictation 46

Don't shout all the time!/ I can hear you/ well enough/ when you speak quietly./ However,/ the best way to learn anything in English/ is by practice./ They've always kept their promises,/ so they say./ Of course he finds life boring;/ he watches the same television programmes/ all the time./ They were nearly blinded/ by the snowstorm,/ and could not see which direction/ the ambulance was coming from.

Do Revision Exercise 30

LESSON 75

397 **look like**

What famous person would you most like to look like? I'd most like to look like ...

What does he/she look like? He/She is ... and has ...

Do you look more like your mother or your father? I look more like my ...

Do you think it looks like rain (or looks as if it is going to rain)? Yes, I think ... ~ No, I don't think ...

Do you think you look like succeeding (or look as if you will succeed) in learning English quite well? Yes, I think I look ...

travel **journey** **just**

The difference between "travel" and "journey" is that we generally use "travel" as a verb and "journey" as a noun. For example, "I travelled a long way" or "The journey was long".

What's the difference between "travel" and "journey"? The difference between ...

Why is it now easier for people to travel to other countries just for the weekend? It's now easier ... because travelling is cheaper and faster these days

398 What's the longest journey you've ever made? The longest journey I've ever made is from ... to ...

of course

Give me a sentence with the words "of course" in it, please. Could I borrow your pen for a second? Of course you can ~ He's American and so, of course, he speaks English

nowadays

Do you think people are happier nowadays than they were in the past?
Yes, I think ... ~ No, I don't think ...

Why or why not?

suffer

Have you suffered from any illnesses in the last two years?
Yes, I've suffered from some illnesses ...
~ No, I haven't suffered from any illnesses ...

wish

What's your greatest wish in life? My greatest wish in life is ...

exist

About how long has this building existed for? This building has existed for ...

399 remind in other words member

The difference between the words "remember" and "remind" is that we remember something ourselves, without help, whereas, if we forget something, somebody reminds us. In other words, they remember for us.

What's the difference between the words "remember" and "remind"?
The difference between ...

If you forget the meaning of a word during the lesson, who reminds you of it? If I forget ..., the teacher reminds me of it

If you have an important appointment to keep, which member of your family reminds you to keep it? If I have ..., my ... reminds me ...

Do I remind you of any member of your family? Yes, you remind me of ... ~ No, you don't remind me of any ...

library

What's the difference between a bookshop and a library?

The difference ... is that a bookshop is a place where we can buy books, whereas a library is a place where we can go to read books and borrow them

even though even not even

When you were a child, did you sometimes have to go to school even though you didn't want to?

Yes, when I was a child, I sometimes had to ... I didn't want to

400 Are there some areas of the world where it never gets warm, even in the middle of summer?

Yes, there are ...

Will there be even more people and more cars in the world in a few years' time?

Yes, there'll be ...

Do you know of a village in this country where they haven't even got water or electricity?

Yes, I know of ... ~ No, I don't know of ...

Where?

to at direction

The difference between the words "to" and "at" is that we generally use "to" when we are moving in the direction of a place, and "at" when we are there. For example, "I'm going to the table. Now, I'm (standing) at the table".

What's the difference between the words "to" and "at"?

The difference between ...

Give me an example, please.

I'm going to the table, and now I'm at the table

Are you coming to the school?

No, I'm not ...; I'm at the school

Am I going to the table?

No, you aren't ...; you're (standing) at the table

soon — at once

If I go out of the room and say "I'll be back soon", how long will I be?
If you go ..., you'll be maybe five or ten minutes

If I go out of the room and say "I'll be back at once", how long will I be?
If you go ..., you'll be about one minute, or you'll be back almost immediately

401 **Will it soon be spring (summer, autumn, or winter)?** Yes, it'll soon be ...

Is the lesson going to finish soon? Yes, the lesson's ... ~ No, the lesson isn't ...

How soon do you think it will be before everybody in the world has enough money in order to live a comfortable life? I think it'll be a long time before everybody ...

Which would get you home sooner: a bus or a car? I think maybe a car would get me home sooner than a bus

LESSON 76

402 **need**

What would you do if you needed a haircut? — If I needed ..., I'd go to a hairdresser's

What do you think you need more than anything else in your life? — I think I need ... more than anything else in my life

What do you think your country needs more than anything else? — I think my country needs ... more than anything else

towards **destination**

The word "towards" means "in the direction of". For example, if I say "I'm walking towards the station" it means that I'm walking in the direction of the station; it doesn't necessarily mean that the station is my destination.

What does the word "towards" mean? — The word "towards" means ...

What am I doing? — You're walking towards the door

If I tell you that I am driving towards Scotland, does that necessarily mean that Scotland is my destination? — No, if you tell me that you are ..., that doesn't necessarily mean that Scotland is your destination

403 **tray**

What do we use a tray for? — We use a tray for carrying plates and cups from one room to another

stadium

Where is the nearest sports stadium? — The nearest ...

About how many people does it hold? — It holds ...

much better **much more**

If we put the word "much" before a comparative, it communicates that the difference between the two things is very big. For example, Germany is bigger than England, but China is much bigger than England.

Why do you speak English much better now than you did six months ago?

I speak English ... than I did six months ago because I've had much more practice

Why is a Rolls Royce much more expensive than an ordinary car?

A Rolls Royce is ... because it takes longer to make than an ordinary car

contrary **fall**

temperature **atmosphere**

What's another word for "opposite"?

Another word for "opposite" is "contrary"

What's the contrary of the verb "to rise"?

"To fall" is the contrary ...

404 Is the temperature of the atmosphere falling this month?

Yes, the temperature ... ~ No, the temperature ...; it's rising

If your body temperature falls a lot, what should you do?

If my body temperature ..., I should go to bed and call a doctor

tooth **teeth** **toothbrush** **dentist**

What's the plural of "tooth"?

The plural of "tooth" is "teeth"

What do we clean our teeth with?

We clean our teeth with a toothbrush

If you have a problem with your teeth, who should you go to see?

If I have ... with my teeth, I should go to see a dentist

seem

Does it seem to you as if it'll rain later?

Yes, it seems to me as if ... ~ No, it doesn't seem to me as if ...

Why do some people seem younger than they really are?
Some people seem ... because of the way they look, the way they talk, the things they do etc.

Does it seem warmer to you today than it was yesterday?
Yes, it seems warmer to me...
~ No, it doesn't seem warmer to me ...

several

Are you ill several times during the year? Yes, I'm ill ...
~ No, I'm not ill ...

405 Do some very rich people have houses in several different countries?
Yes, some very ...

compose be composed of

Did Mozart compose a lot of music? Yes, Mozart composed ...

Do you find it difficult to compose formal letters? Yes, I find it ...
~ No, I don't find it ...; I find it easy

How many letters is the English alphabet composed of? The English alphabet is composed of 26 letters

Is Europe composed of many different countries? Yes, Europe's composed of ...

wise wisdom

Do you agree that it's wise to put some money in the bank each month for later on in life? Yes, I agree ...; No, I don't agree ...

Do you think wisdom comes more with age or experience?
I think wisdom comes more with ...

suddenly

If I suddenly threw my pen at you, would you be able to catch it?
Yes, if you ... your pen at me, I'd ...
~ No, if you ... your pen at me, I wouldn't ...

pain

What's the greatest physical pain you've ever suffered?

The greatest ... I've ever suffered was ...

406 ## certain

Is there anything in life that we can be completely certain of?

Yes, there's ... ~ No, there isn't ...

What?

pass by

From where you're sitting can you see people passing by the window?

Yes, from where I'm sitting, I can ...
~ No, from where I'm sitting, I can't ...

park car park

When a car park is full, where does a driver have to park his car ?

When a ..., a driver ... in the street

picture

Dictation 47

Instead of a belt/ she wore a chain,/ which was the fashion of the day./We usually picture the devil/ as having long ears/ that become thin and narrow/at the top./ The word "great" generally means very good,/ but it can also mean/ big or important./ "Fast" means the same as "quick",/ except that/ we do not add "ly" to it/ as an adverb.

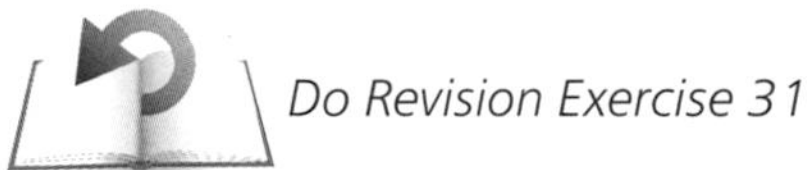

Do Revision Exercise 31

LESSON 77

407 **3rd Conditional**

Before we think about the 3rd conditional, we should remind ourselves of the 1st conditional and 2nd conditional:

1st Conditional

"If" + present + "will do" = real possibility

If I go to the park tomorrow, I will play football

2nd Conditional

"If" + past + "would do" = only imagining

If I went to the park tomorrow, I would play football

When do we use the 1st conditional? — We use the 1st conditional to communicate that we think something is a real possibility in the future

What is its construction? — Its construction is "If" + present + "will do"

Give me an example, please. — If he sees his friend this evening, he will say "Hello"

408 When do we use the 2nd conditional? — We use the 2nd conditional to communicate that we are only imagining something

What is its construction? — Its construction is "If" + past + "would do"

Give me an example, please. — If she went to the North Pole next week, she would feel very cold

3rd Conditional

"If" + past perfect + "would have done"
= imagining in the past

If I had gone to the park yesterday, I would have played football

We use the 3rd conditional to communicate that we are imagining something in the past that did not really happen. Its construction is "If" + past perfect + "would have done". The sentence "If I had gone to the park yesterday, I would have played football" means that, in fact, I did not go to the park yesterday, and I did not play football; I am only imagining.

When do we use the 3rd conditional? We use the 3rd conditional when we are imagining something in the past that did not really happen

What is its construction? Its construction is "If" + past perfect + "would have done"

Give me an example, please. If she had studied harder, she would have succeeded in the exam last month

Notice that, in the 3rd conditional, we put the word "have" and the past participle after the word "would". For example, we say "I would have taken"; "you would have taken"; "he would have taken" etc.

409 In the 3rd conditional, what do we put after the word "would"? In the 3rd conditional, we put the word "have" and the past participle after the word "would"

Give me some examples, please. He would have slept. She would have written. They would have eaten.

If you had been born in England, which language would you have spoken as a child? If I had been ..., I would have spoken English as a child

Were you in fact born in England? No, I wasn't in fact ...; I was born in ...

Exactly; we are only imagining.

Did you find £100 on the street yesterday? No, I didn't ...

But if you had found £100 on the street yesterday, what would you have done with it?

If I had ..., I would have kept it/taken it to the police station

If you had not decided to study English, which language would you have studied instead?

If I had not ..., I would have studied ... instead

If you had not come to school last week, what would you have done instead?

If I had not ..., I would have gone on holiday/stayed at home etc.

diary

What do people use diaries for?

People use diaries to help them remember things that they have done or things that they need to do

410 character

What kind of character do you like to see in a person?

I like to see a ... character in a person

really

Have you ever got up really early?

Yes, I've sometimes ... ~ No, I've never ...

For what reason?

If you were driving a car on a long journey and suddenly felt really tired, what would you do?

If I were ..., I'd stop the car, buy a cup of coffee, and wait until I felt more awake

ran

What's the past of "run"?

The past of ... "ran"

If you ran against him (or me etc.), who do you think'd win?

If I ran ..., I think ... would win

improve coach

How can we improve our English?

We can ... by practising a lot, reading a lot etc.

Why do even the best tennis players need a coach? Even the best ... to help them to improve their game

Is it cheaper to travel by coach or by train in your country? It's cheaper ... in my country

411 Adverbs formed from adjectives

As you have already seen, one very common way of forming adverbs is by adding the letters "ly" to the adjective. For example, "careful – carefully"; "dangerous – dangerously"; "useless – uselessly" etc.

Tell me one very common way of forming adverbs from adjectives? One very common way ...

Give me some examples, please. bad – badly; quick – quickly etc.

flew

What's the past of "fly"? The past of "fly" is "flew"

If you flew round the world in a straight line, would you finish in the same place as you had started? Yes, if I flew ..., I'd finish in ...

If a bird flew into this room, what'd you do? If a bird ..., I'd probably try to catch it

wool

Which animal do we get wool from? We get wool from a sheep

What can we make from wool? We can make pullovers, hats and scarves from wool

412 Possessive case of plural nouns ending in "s"

apostrophe case

How do we form the possessive case of singular nouns like "girl", "man", "child" etc.? We form the possessive case of ... by adding an apostrophe and the letter "s"

Give me some examples, please.

The girl's coat; the old man's hat; a child's book

How do we form the possessive case of plural nouns that do not end in "s", such as "men", "women", "children" etc.?

We form the possessive case of ... in the same way: by adding an apostrophe and the letter "s"

Give me some examples, please.

The old men's hats; children's books; women's clothes

When, however, a plural noun already ends in "s", we form its possessive case just by adding an apostrophe, but no "s".

How do we form the possessive case of a plural noun which already ends in "s"?

We form the possessive case of ... just by adding an apostrophe, but no "s"

Give me some examples, please.

The girls' coats; the workers' clothes; ladies' dresses

What do footballers' shirts have written on their backs?

Footballers' shirts have numbers written on their backs

kick

What am I doing?

You're kicking the table

413 coast certain

Can the English coast be seen from the coast of France?

Yes, on certain days, the English coast ...

tire

Do you ever tire of speaking?

Yes, I sometimes tire ... ~ No, I never tire ...

Dictation 48

What have they just done?/ They've just learnt that/ we use the first conditional/ to communicate that we think/ something is a real possibility./ Its construction is/ "if" + present + "will do"./ In the second conditional,/ we use the past tense to communicate/ that we are only imagining something./ We use "would"/ followed by the infinitive without "to"/ to talk about the imagined result.

Revision Exercise 24 (Lessons 52 – 53)

1 Which do you prefer: cats or dogs?

2 Do people in your country think it's lucky to see a black cat?

3 Do you ever destroy documents that you receive from your bank?

4 Have you been to the cinema this week?

5 Have you ever been to Scotland?

6 If I take something from a shop without paying, am I guilty of a crime?

7 What's the opposite of "guilty"?

8 Have you visited Paris?

9 Are you too short to touch the ceiling?

10 If you work too much, do you feel tired all the time?

11 At what age did you begin school?

12 How much does the average meal cost in the average restaurant in the place where you live?

13 Is your book thinner than the glass in the window?

14 Is Switzerland a bigger country than India?

15 What's the difference between a purse and a wallet?

16 Which do you think it's worse to lose, your keys or your purse/wallet?

17 Do you find English easy to learn?

18 What kind of things make you angry?

19 What does it mean "to swim like a fish"?

20 What do we call the two ends of a swimming pool?

Answers

1 I prefer ...

2 Yes, people in my country think it's lucky to see a black cat. ~ No, people in my country don't think it's lucky to see a black cat; they think it's unlucky.

3 Yes, I sometimes destroy documents that I receive from my bank.

4 Yes, I've been to the cinema this week. ~ No, I haven't been to the cinema this week.

5 Yes, I've been to Scotland. ~ No, I've never been to Scotland.

6 Yes, if you take something from a shop without paying, you're guilty of a crime.

7 The opposite of "guilty" is "innocent".

8 Yes, I have visited Paris. ~ No, I haven't visited Paris.

9 Yes, I'm too short to touch the ceiling.

10 Yes, if I work too much, I feel tired all the time.

11 I began school at the age of ...

12 The average meal costs about ... in the average restaurant in the place where I live.

13 No, my book isn't thinner than the glass in the window; it's thicker.

14 No, Switzerland isn't a bigger country than India; it's a smaller country than India.

15 The difference between a purse and a wallet is that women generally have purses and men generally have wallets.

16 I think it's worse to lose my ...

17 Yes, I find English easy to learn. ~ No, I don't find English easy to learn; I find it difficult.

18 The kind of things that make me angry are when things go wrong, when people are making too much noise ... etc.

19 "To swim like a fish" means to be a strong swimmer.

20 We call the two ends of a swimming pool the shallow end and the deep end.

Revision Exercise 25 (Lessons 54 – 55)

1 What do we call a bad dream?

2 Do you ever refuse to help other people?

3 Do you live in a separate house from your parents?

4 Do you agree it's very bad for the health to keep eating after our stomachs are completely full?

5 Do you keep your money in your pocket, or do you use a purse or wallet?

6 Do you keep books after you've read them?

7 What's the best way to keep warm on a cold day?

8 What do we sometimes mean when we use the words "one, you, we" and "they"?

9 What do you have to do if you want to stay healthy?

10 Which country must we go to if we want to hear people speaking Greek?

11 What's the difference between the present perfect and the past simple?

12 Have you been to the cinema this year?

13 When was the last time you went to the cinema?

14 Does your bank have a branch near here?

15 Are there any bridges over the river in Paris?

16 What subject interests you the most?

17 Are you interested in the history of your country?

18 Do you get bored if you have nothing to do?

19 What's the difference between "between" and "among"?

20 Among all the places you've ever been to, which do you think is the ugliest?

Answers

1 We call a bad dream a nightmare.

2 Yes, I sometimes refuse to help other people. ~ No, I never refuse to help other people.

3 Yes, I live in a separate house from my parents. ~ No, I don't live in a separate house from my parents; I live in the same house.

4 Yes, I agree it's very bad for the health to keep eating after our stomachs are completely full.

5 Yes, I keep my money in my pocket. ~ No, I don't keep my money in my pocket; I use a purse/wallet.

6 Yes, I keep books after I've read them. ~ No, I don't keep books after I've read them.

7 The best way to keep warm on a cold day is to wear a thick coat.

8 When we use the words "one, you, we" and "they" we sometimes mean people in general.

9 If you want to stay healthy, you have to eat healthy food, sleep well and do exercise.

10 We must go to Greece if we want to hear people speaking Greek.

11 The difference between the present perfect and the past simple is that we use the present perfect when we are thinking about time before or up to now, whereas we use the past simple when we are thinking about a specific past time.

12 Yes, I've been to the cinema this year. ~ No, I haven't been to the cinema this year.

13 The last time I went to the cinema was ...

14 Yes, my bank has a branch near here. ~ No, my bank doesn't have a branch near here.

15 Yes, there are some bridges over the river in Paris.

16 ... interests me the most.

17 Yes, I'm interested in the history of my country. ~ No, I'm not interested in the history of my country.

18 Yes, I get bored if I have nothing to do. ~ No, I don't get bored if I have nothing to do.

19 The difference between "between" and "among" is that we generally use "between" for two people or things, whilst we use "among" for more than two people or things.

20 Among all the places I've ever been to, I think ... is the ugliest.

Revision Exercise 26 (Lessons 56 – 57)

1 Do you think it's going to rain soon?

2 What kind of things do you enjoy doing most of all?

3 Do you always enjoy your weekends?

4 What kind of hole do we find in a door?

5 Which do you think are more intelligent: cats or dogs?

6 What's another word for "intelligent"?

7 Who does your town play football against?

8 What's the past participle of the verb "to go"?

9 Why can I say "Mr Brown has gone to Scotland", but not "I have gone to Scotland"?

10 Can a bird fly quicker than a plane (aeroplane)?

11 What's the difference between "thick" and "fat"?

12 Did you swim last summer?

13 Have you ever lost your way in a large city?

14 What's the difference between "each other" and "one another"?

15 Do your country and England play football against each other?

16 Do the countries of Europe do business with one another?

17 What's the past of "can"?

18 What's the future of "can"?

19 Tell me the names of some things that we make in factories.

20 Do soldiers wear ordinary clothes?

Answers

1 Yes, I think it's going to rain soon. ~ No, I don't think it's going to rain soon.

2 The kind of things I enjoy doing most of all are watching television, going to the cinema etc.

3 Yes, I always enjoy my weekends. ~ No, I don't always enjoy my weekends.

4 We find a keyhole in a door.

5 I think ... are more intelligent than ...

6 Another word for "intelligent" is "clever".

7 My town plays football against ...

8 The past participle of the verb "to go" is "gone".

9 I can say "Mr Brown has gone to Scotland", but not "I have gone to Scotland", because "I have gone to Scotland" means I am not here now, which is impossible.

10 No, a bird can't fly quicker than a plane; it flies slower than a plane (aeroplane).

11 The difference between "thick" and "fat" is that we use "thick" for things and "fat" for people and animals.

12 Yes, I swam last summer. ~ No, I didn't swim last summer.

13 Yes, I've sometimes lost my way in a large city. ~ No, I've never lost my way in a large city.

14 The difference between each other and one another is that we generally use "each other" for two people or things, and "one another" for more than two people or things.

15 Yes, my country and England play football against each other. ~ No, my country and England don't play football against each other.

16 Yes, the countries of Europe do business with one another.

17 The past of "can" is "could".

18 "Can" has no future. Therefore, we use the verb "to be able" and say "I will be able".

19 The names of some things that we make in factories are cars, pens etc.

20 No, soldiers don't wear ordinary clothes; they wear uniforms.

Revision Exercise 27 (Lessons 58 – 59)

1 Can you understand all the words when you listen to a song in English?

2 What's the difference between the words "fun" and "funny"?

3 Have you had your lunch today?

4 What's the furthest you've ever swum?

5 Is it possible to learn English simply by listening to English songs?

6 Have you ever taken things that weren't yours by mistake?

7 What's the difference between these two sentences? "I'm going to buy the car if it's cheap" and "I'm going to buy the car whether it's cheap or not?

8 What is the highest speed a car can go when in town in this country?

9 Do you like unpleasant surprises?

10 Is it a big struggle for you to get up on a cold winter's morning when you feel very tired?

11 Do you think computers make your life easier or more difficult?

12 Do you turn off your computer when you go to bed at night?

13 Tell me the names of some great people in history.

14 What is the past simple and the past participle of the verb "to keep"?

15 Have you always kept your promises?

16 Did you find English very difficult when you began studying it?

17 Have you ever found anything on the street worth a lot of money?

18 Does anybody else in your family speak English besides you?

19 Is it easier to dance well if you have a good sense of rhythm?

20 When somebody makes you angry, do you say something or do you just stay quiet?

Answers

1 No, I can't understand all the words when I listen to a song in English.

2 The difference between the words "fun" and "funny" is that, if something is fun, we enjoy it, whereas, if something is funny, it makes us laugh.

3 Yes, I've had my lunch today. ~ No, I haven't had my lunch today.

4 The furthest I've ever swum is ...

5 No, it isn't possible to learn English simply by listening to English songs.

6 Yes, I've sometimes taken things that weren't mine by mistake. ~ No, I've never taken things that weren't mine by mistake.

7 The difference between these two sentences is that the first sentence means I'm going to buy the car only if it's cheap, whereas the second sentence means I'm going to buy the car if it's cheap or expensive; the price is not important.

8 The highest speed a car can go when in town in this country is ...

9 No, I don't like unpleasant surprises.

10 Yes, it's a big struggle for me to get up on a cold winter's morning when I feel very tired.

11 I think computers make my life ...

12 Yes, I turn off my computer when I go to bed at night. ~ No, I don't turn off my computer when I go to bed at night.

13 The names of some great people in history are Mahatma Gandhi, Albert Einstein, Marie Curie etc.

14 The past simple and the past participle of the verb "to keep" is "kept".

15 Yes, I've always kept my promises. ~ No, I haven't always kept my promises; sometimes I've broken them.

16 Yes, I found English very difficult when I began studying it.

17 Yes, I've found something on the street worth a lot of money. ~ No, I've never found anything on the street worth a lot of money.

18 Yes, somebody else in my family speaks English besides me. ~ No, nobody else in my family speaks English besides me.

19 Yes, it's easier to dance well if you have a good sense of rhythm.

20 When somebody makes me angry, I ...

Revision Exercise 28 (Lesson 60 – 61)

1 Is it probable that it will snow next summer?

2 When do we use the 1st conditional?

3 When do we use the 2nd conditional?

4 If you felt ill tomorrow, would you go out?

5 If you study hard, will you learn to speak English well?

6 If you had £1 million, what would you buy?

7 If you swam in the sea in the middle of winter, would you find the water warm?

8 If you go on holiday next year, where will you go?

9 If you found something in the street worth a lot of money, would you keep it or would you take it to the police station?

10 If you sent a letter and forgot to put the address on it, would it arrive?

11 Do you prefer chatting with your friends on the phone or online?

12 What's the first thing you notice about people when you meet them for the first time?

13 Is it more comfortable to sleep lying down or sitting up?

14 What was the first thing you saw when you woke up today?

15 If you went from London to Rome, which cities would you perhaps have to go through?

16 When a teacher puts a cross next to an answer in a written test, what does it mean?

17 Is it dangerous to drive after drinking alcohol?

18 What's the difference between these two sentences: "I must study" and "I should study"?

19 In a Callan Method lesson, does the teacher correct your grammatical mistakes?

20 If you have a problem with a colleague at work, should you speak to your boss about it?

Answers

1 No, it isn't probable that it will snow next summer; it's very improbable.

2 We use the 1st conditional to communicate that we think something is a real possibility.

3 We use the 2nd conditional to communicate that we are only imagining something.

4 No, if I felt ill tomorrow, I wouldn't go out; I would stay at home.

5 Yes, if I study hard, I will learn to speak English well.

6 If I had £1 million, I would buy ...

7 No, if I swam in the sea in the middle of winter, I wouldn't find the water warm; I would find it cold.

8 If I go on holiday next year, I will go to ...

9 If I found something in the street worth a lot of money, I would keep it/take it to the police station.

10 No, if I sent a letter and forgot to put the address on it, it wouldn't arrive.

11 I prefer chatting with my friends ...

12 The first thing I notice about people when I meet them for the first time is their voice (clothes, eyes etc.)

13 It's more comfortable to sleep lying down than sitting up.

14 The first thing I saw when I woke up today was ...

15 If I went from London to Rome, I would perhaps have to go through Paris, Milan etc.

16 When a teacher puts a cross next to an answer in a written test, it means the answer is wrong.

17 Yes, it's dangerous to drive after drinking alcohol.

18 The difference between those two sentences is that "I must study" means that I have no alternative, whereas "I should study" means I have alternatives but that studying is the right thing for me to do.

19 Yes, in a Callan Method lesson, the teacher corrects your grammatical mistakes

20 Yes, if I have a problem with a colleague at work, I should speak to my boss about it.

Revision Exercise 29 (Lessons 62 – 63)

1 Do you think the lives of the poor are happier than those of the rich?

2 Although you're now able to hold a simple conversation in English, do you think you should keep studying?

3 Does your mum cook tasty food?

4 Give me a sentence with the words "such as" in it.

5 If a factory belonged to you, do you think you would be able to make a lot of money?

6 If you were a doctor, would you be able to help people who were ill?

7 Is Napoleon alive?

8 What happened to President Kennedy?

9 Is it usual for people in your country to eat hot food for breakfast?

10 What's the difference between "still" and "yet"?

11 When our shoes are dirty, what should we do?

12 Would you be afraid to go round the world in a small open boat?

13 What's the best way to guard against becoming ill?

14 What's the best way to calm somebody down when he's very angry?

15 If you were a millionaire, where would you live?

16 If you were a king, what would your wife be called?

17 When do we say "if I were you, ..."?

18 If you won a million pounds, what would you do with it?

19 What do we do with useless things?

20 Do you think that what you're learning now will be useful to you later on in life?

Answers

1 Yes, I think the lives of the poor are happier than those of the rich. ~ No, I don't think the lives of the poor are happier than those of the rich. I think they're less happy.

2 Yes, although I'm now able to hold a simple conversation in English, I think I should keep studying.

3 Yes, my mum cooks tasty food. ~ No, my mum doesn't cook tasty food.

4 I like reading all kinds of books, such as history books, science books etc.

5 Yes, if a factory belonged to me, I think I would be able to make a lot of money.

6 Yes, if I were a doctor, I could help people who were ill.

7 No, Napoleon isn't alive; he's dead.

8 President Kennedy was assassinated (in 1963).

9 Yes, it's usual for people in my country to eat hot food for breakfast. ~ No, it isn't usual for people in my country to eat hot food for breakfast.

10 The difference between "still" and "yet" is that we use "still" for something that is in progress at the moment, whereas we use "yet" for something that has not begun or happened. We generally use "still" in positive sentences, whereas we generally use "yet" in questions and negative sentences.

11 When our shoes are dirty, we should clean them.

12 Yes, I would be afraid to go round the world in a small open boat. ~ No, I wouldn't be afraid to go round the world in a small open boat.

13 The best way to guard against becoming ill is to eat healthy food, sleep well and do exercise.

14 The best way to calm somebody down when he's very angry is to speak quietly and pleasantly to him.

15 If I were a millionaire, I would live in ...

16 If I were a king, my wife would be called a queen.

17 We say "If I were you, ...", when we want to give advice to somebody, especially when we think perhaps there is a problem.

18 If I won ..., I would ...

19 We throw useless things away.

20 Yes, I think that what I'm learning now will be useful to me later on in life.

Revision Exercise 30 (Lessons 64 - 65)

1 If a plant had no water, would it die?

2 If today were Sunday, what'd tomorrow be?

3 What kind of things do we put in sandwiches?

4 Are your dictations usually faultless?

5 What must two people or things have if we want to make a comparison between them?

6 Give me a sentence with "even" in it.

7 If you mixed some red and white paint together, what would you get?

8 Do you take good care of your health?

9 Would you take your time going home if somebody told you your house was on fire?

10 Do people hurry when they have plenty of time?

11 What's the difference between "for" and "since"?

12 Why do people use microwaves instead of normal cookers?

13 Do you hope your English studies will help your future career?

14 If you lent something to somebody and they didn't return it, what'd you do?

15 What's a film star?

16 What's the most agricultural region of your country?

17 If you keep somebody waiting for a long time, should you apologise?

18 How can we help to avoid becoming ill?

19 Do you like the fashion in clothes at the moment?

20 Why should you not worry if you don't immediately understand some of the grammar in this book?

Answers

1 Yes, if a plant had no water, it would die.

2 If today were Sunday, tomorrow'd be Monday.

3 We put meat, cheese, egg etc. in sandwiches.

4 No, my dictations aren't usually faultless; they usually contain mistakes.

5 If we want to make a comparison between two people or things, they must have something in common.

6 She speaks Russian, German, French, and even Chinese. ~

7 If I mixed some red and white paint together, I'd get pink paint.

8 Yes, I take good care of my health ~ No, I don't take good care of my health.

9 No, I wouldn't take my time going home if somebody told me my house was on fire; I'd hurry.

10 No, people don't hurry when they have plenty of time; they take their time.

11 The difference between "for" and "since" is that we use the word "for" when we say a period of time, whereas we use the word "since" when we say the point at which the period began.

12 People use microwaves instead of normal cookers because microwaves cook food more quickly than normal cookers.

13 Yes, I hope my English studies will help my future career.

14 If I lent something to somebody and they didn't return it, I'd ...

15 A film star is a famous actor or actress in the cinema world.

16 ... is the most agricultural region of my country.

17 Yes, if you keep somebody waiting for a long time, you should apologise.

18 We can help to avoid becoming ill by living a healthy life.

19 Yes, I like the fashion in clothes at the moment. ~ No, I don't like the fashion in clothes at the moment.

20 I shouldn't worry if I don't immediately understand some of the grammar in this book because I will practise it again in other lessons, and I can study it at home.

Revision Exercise 31 (Lessons 66 – 67)

1 What were you doing at this time last Sunday?

2 About how much does a doctor earn a year in your country?

3 What does a man wear when he goes to a formal dinner?

4 How often do you go to the hairdresser's?

5 Why do you think some films are so popular?

6 What does a bathroom usually contain?

7 What does a mirror do?

8 How do we form the passive voice?

9 Now I am going to give you a sentence in the active voice, and I want you to put it into the passive voice: John ate the pasta.

10 Now I am going to give you a sentence in the active voice, and I want you to put it into the passive voice: My boss is going to write that email.

11 When you were a child, did your parents make you eat your vegetables?

12 Which would you prefer as a snack during a morning break: a bag of crisps or some biscuits?

13 How soon after you were born did you learn to walk?

14 What do we call the part of a tree that's in the land?

15 If you wanted to go from here to Scotland, would you have to cross the sea or would you be able to go all the way by land?

16 Is it safe for young children to cross the road on their own?

17 How long did you lie in bed for last night?

18 When do people use the words "sir" and "madam"?

19 When do we use the words "gentleman" and "lady"?

20 What's the standard height for a man (or woman) in your country?

Answers

1 I was ... at this time last Sunday.

2 A doctor earns about ... a year in my country.

3 A man wears a suit and tie when he goes to a formal dinner.

4 I go to the hairdresser's ... times a year.

5 I think some films are so popular because they tell interesting or exciting stories.

6 A bathroom usually contains a toilet, a basin, and a bath or shower.

7 A mirror reflects light.

8 We form the passive voice with the verb "to be" and a past participle.

9 The pasta was eaten by John.

10 That email is going to be written by my boss.

11 Yes, when I was a child, my parents made me eat my vegetables. ~ No, when I was a child, my parents didn't make me eat my vegetables.

12 I'd prefer ... as a snack during a morning break.

13 I learnt to walk about a year after I was born.

14 We call the part of a tree that's in the land the roots.

15 If I wanted to go from here to Scotland, I'd ...

16 No, it isn't safe for young children to cross the road on their own.

17 I lay in bed for ... hours last night.

18 People use the words "sir" and "madam" to be polite when they speak to customers.

19 We use the words "gentleman" and "lady" instead of "man" and "woman" when we want to sound polite.

20 The standard height for a man/woman in my country is ...

INDEX

Index

STAGE 5 VOCABULARY

Arabic Vocabulary

LESSON 61

315	chat	يدردش
315	online	عبر شبكة الإنترنت
315	notice	يلاحظ
315	free	غير مشغول/مجاني
315	busy	مشغول
316	lie	يطرح
316	comfortable	مريح
316	uncomfortable	غير مريح
316	pillow	وسادة
316	wake up - woke up - woken up	يستيقظ - استيقظ - استيقظ
316	go to sleep	يذهب للنوم
316	immediately	على الفور
316	midnight	منتصف الليل
317	through	عبر
317	button	زر
317	buttonhole	عروة
317	career	مسار وظيفي
317	cross	تقاطع
317	crossroads	تقاطع الطرق
317	test	اختبار
318	danger	خطر
318	dangerous	خطير
318	dangerously	بشكل خطير
318	alcohol	كحول
318	detective	مخبر سري
318	should	ينبغي
318	obligation	التزام
318	alternative	بديل
318	ambulance	سيارة الإسعاف
319	correct	يصحح
319	grammatical	نحوي
319	problem	مشكلة
319	cause	سبب/قضية
319	colleague	زميل
319	boss	رئيس
319	freedom	حرية
319	justice	عدالة
320	as	بما أن
320	that is	أي
320	bone	عظم

LESSON 62

322	life	حياة
322	lives	حياة/أرواح
322	the poor	الفقراء
322	the rich	الأغنياء
322	although	على الرغم
322	cook	يطبخ/طباخ
322	tasty	حلو المذاق
322	pasta	باستا
323	independent	مستقل
323	origin	أصل
323	belong to	يخص
323	could	استطاع/ كان سيستطيع
323	vice versa	العكس بالعكس
324	throw	يلقي
324	alive	حي
324	dead	ميت
324	drop	يُسقِط/يسقط
324	go without	يحرم من
325	assassinate	يغتال
325	usual	المعتاد
325	unusual	غير المعتاد
325	still	لا يزال
325	yet	بعد
325	in progress	قيد العمل
326	special	خاص

LESSON 63

327	clean	نظيف
327	dirty	متسخ
327	dirt	الأوساخ
327	know of	يعرف بـ
327	to be afraid	يخاف من
328	guard	يحمي من
328	on your guard	توخى الحذر
328	off your guard	لا تتوخ الحذر
328	calm	يهدئ/هادئ
328	quietly	بهدوء
328	if I were	لو كنت ...
328	king	ملك
328	person (1st, 2nd person etc.)	المتكلم/المخاطب إلخ
329	if I were you, ...	لو كنت محلك، ...
329	advice	نصيحة
329	expression	عبارة
329	especially	خاصة
330	win - won - won	يفوز - فاز - فاز
330	lottery	يانصيب
330	useful	مفيد
330	useless	لا فائدة منه
330	possess	يمتلك
331	take by surprise	يفاجئ

LESSON 64

332	contract	يختصر
333	sandwich	شطيرة
333	cheese	الجبن
333	fault	خطأ
333	faultless	لا عيب فيه
333	faulty	متعطل
333	fix	يصلح
334	OK	حسنا
334	all right	حسنًا
334	compare	يقارن
334	comparison	مقارنة
334	have something in common	لديهم شيء مشترك
334	ice	الثلج
334	cool	منعش
334	pour	يصب
335	unite	يتحد
335	even	حتى
335	surprising	مفاجئ
335	mix	يخلط
335	mixture	خليط
335	pink	زهري
335	care	عناية/يهتم
335	care for	يعتني بـ
335	take care of	اعتن بـ
336	appointment	موعد
336	keep an appointment	يوفي بموعده

336 hurry .... يستعجل
336 take your time .... خذ وقتك
336 plenty of .... الكثير من

LESSON 65

338 for .... لمدة
338 since .... منذ
338 period .... فترة
338 point .... نقطة
339 kitchen .... مطبخ
339 fridge .... ثلاجة
339 freezer .... مجمد
339 cooker .... موقد
339 sink .... حوض
339 microwave .... فرن الميكرويف
339 studies .... دراسات
340 lend - lent - lent .... يقرض - أقرض - أقرض
340 return .... يعيد
340 first name .... الاسم الأول
340 surname .... اسم العائلة
340 actor .... ممثل
340 actress .... ممثلة
340 famous .... مشهور
340 film star .... نجم السينما
341 industrial .... صناعي
341 agricultural .... زراعي
341 region .... منطقة
341 apologize .... يعتذر
341 apology .... اعتذار
341 keep somebody waiting... يبقي شخص ما منتظرًا
341 avoid .... تجنب
341 bend .... ينحني
342 century .... قرن
342 fashion .... موضة
342 gate .... بوابة
342 worry .... يقلق
342 be worried .... يشعر بالقلق
342 run .... يركض

LESSON 66

344 I was speaking .... كنت أتحدث
344 particular .... معين
344 while .... بينما
345 earn .... يكسب
345 formal .... رسمي
345 informal .... غير رسمي
345 jeans .... جينز
345 trainer .... حذاء رياضي
345 how do you do? .... كيف حالكم؟
346 persuade .... يقنع
346 hairdresser .... حلاق
346 so = very .... كثيرًا = جدًا
346 interesting .... شيق
346 exciting .... مثير
346 grammatically .... نحويًا
346 bathroom .... غرفة الحمام
346 bath .... بانيو
346 shower .... دش
346 toilet .... مرحاض
346 basin .... حوض
347 mirror .... مرآة
347 reflect .... يعكس
347 active .... معلوم
347 passive .... مجهول
347 subject .... فاعل
347 object .... مفعول به
348 by .... من قبل

LESSON 67

350 force .... يجبر
350 make somebody do .... يجعل شخص ما يفعل ...
350 snack .... وجبة خفيفة
350 break .... استراحة
350 biscuit .... بسكويت
350 crisps .... رقائق البطاطس
350 to be born .... أن يولد
351 murder .... جريمة قتل
351 prison .... سجن
351 pupil .... تلميذ
351 root .... جذر
351 memory .... ذاكرة
352 cross .... يعبر
353 think of .... يفكر في
353 safe .... آمن
353 safety .... السلامة
353 on your own .... بمفردك
353 lay .... استلقى
354 sir .... السيد
354 madam .... السيدة
354 gentleman .... جنتلمان
354 lady .... السيدة
354 customer .... عميل
354 officer .... ضابط
354 title .... لقب
355 standard .... مستوى/قياسي
355 height .... طول
355 colourful .... غني بالألوان

LESSON 68

356 would you say .... هل تعتقد
356 opinion .... رأي
357 get in .... يركب
357 get out of .... ينزل من
357 get on .... يركب
357 get off .... ينزل من
357 taxi .... سيارة أجرة
357 fare .... أجرة
357 royal .... ملكي
357 mud .... طين
357 countryside .... الريف
357 crowd .... الجمهور
357 crowded .... مزدحم
358 captain .... قبطان
358 team .... فريق
358 wide .... عريض
358 narrow .... ضيق
358 flag .... علم
358 national .... وطني
358 grass .... عشب
358 live on .... يعيش على
359 tower .... برج
359 wet .... مبلل
359 dry .... جاف
359 threw .... ألقى
359 loud .... ذو صوت مرتفع
359 turn up .... يرفع
359 turn down .... يخفض
360 myself .... نفسي
360 yourself .... نفسك
360 himself .... نفسه
360 herself .... نفسها
360 itself .... (نفسه (لغير العاقل
360 oneself .... نفسه
360 ourselves .... أنفسنا
360 yourselves .... أنفسكم
360 themselves .... أنفسهم

360	consequently	وبالتالي
360	protect	يحمي

LESSON 69

362	thorough	دقيق
362	thoroughly	بشكل دقيق
362	accident	حادث
362	by accident	بالصدفة
363	careful	حذر
363	careless	غير متقن
363	carefully	بعناية
363	carelessly	بإهمال
363	own	يملك
363	carry on	يستمر
363	retire	يتقاعد
364	prize	جائزة
364	too	أيضًا
364	at least	على الأقل
364	widely	على نطاق واسع
364	manner	أسلوب
364	pig	خنزير
365	asleep	نائم
365	awake	مستيقظ
365	hospital	مستشفى
365	nurse	ممرض
365	purpose	هدف
365	in order to ...	لكي ...
365	so that	لكي
365	take exercise	يمارس التمارين الرياضية
366	notice	إشعار
366	lain	قد استلقى
367	point at	يشير إلى
367	point out	يعلق
367	indicate	يشير
367	grave	قبر
368	neck	رقبة
368	flame	لهب
368	flight	رحلة جوية
368	soup	حساء
368	except	ما عدا

LESSON 70

369	may	ربما
369	might	قد
369	palace	قصر
369	parliament	البرلمان
370	arrive at	يصل إلى
370	point	نقطة
370	arrive in	يصل إلى
370	area	منطقة
370	airport	مطار
370	passport	جواز سفر
370	café	مقهى
370	owe	مدين
370	souvenir	تذْكار
371	pride	افتخار
371	proud	فخور
371	normal	طبيعي
371	normally	بشكل طبيعي
371	take pride in	يفتخر بـ
	servant	خادم
372	wheel	عجلة
372	lorry	شاحنة
372	arrow	سهم
372	centimetre	سنتيمتر
372	metre	متر
372	beard	لحية
372	true	حقيقي/صحيح
372	false	خطأ
372	paper (newspaper)	صحيفة (جريدة)
372	maintain	ينفق
373	it takes	يستغرق
373	Ireland	أيرلندا
373	amount	مبلغ
373	amount to	يساوي
373	further	أبعد/فضلاً عن/المزيد
373	Sweden	السويد
373	in addition	بالإضافة إلى ذلك
373	extra	إضافي

LESSON 71

375	I had eaten	كنت قد أكلت
376	party	حفل/حزب/مجموعة
376	political	سياسي
377	mad	غاضب/شغف بـ/مجنون
377	crazy	مجنون
377	UFO	جسم طائر لا يمكن تحديد هويته
377	copy	ينسخ/نسخة
378	influence	أثر
378	mouse	فأر
378	mice	فئران
378	throat	حلق
378	opportunity	فرصة
378	develop	يطور
378	industry	صناعة
378	agriculture	زراعة
379	print	طباعة
379	sand	رمل
379	beach	شاطئ
379	desert	صحراء
379	bell	جرس
379	knock	يطرق
379	pay a visit	يقوم بزيارة
379	ring	يرن
379	shout	صراخ/يصرخ
380	stick	عصا
380	walking stick	عصا للمشي
380	exclamation mark	علامة التعجب

LESSON 72

381	reason	السبب
381	illness	المرض
381	tiredness	التعب
381	darkness	الظلام
381	alone	وحيدًا/وحده
382	already	بالفعل
382	thrown	قد ألقى
382	in spite of	بالرغم من
382	despite	بالرغم من
383	anyone	أي أحد
383	someone	شخص ما
383	no one (no-one)	لا أحد
384	borrow	يقترض
384	my own	الخاص بي
384	emphasize	يؤكد
384	skin	جلد
385	wire	سلك
385	electricity	الكهرباء
385	connection	التوصيل
385	wireless	لاسلكي
385	Wi-Fi	الاتصال اللاسلكي بشبكة الإنترنت
385	hyphen	شرطة
385	boil	يغلي
385	fry	يقلي
385	roast	يشوي
385	brick	الطوب
386	as well	كما هو
386	too	أيضًا

386 also ... أيضًا

LESSON 73

387 I will be speaking ... سوف أتحدث
387 inch ... بوصة
387 foot ... قدم
387 yard ... ياردة
388 chain ... سلسلة
388 rise ... يرتفع
388 constantly ... باستمرار
389 belt ... حزام
389 hourly ... كل ساعة
389 daily ... يومياً
389 weekly ... أسبوعيًا
389 monthly ... شهريًا
389 yearly ... سنويًا
390 allow ... يسمح
390 let – let – let ... يسمح - سمح - سمح
390 everyday ... كل يوم

LESSON 74

392 anywhere ... أي مكان
392 somewhere ... في مكان ما
392 not anywhere ... ليس في أي مكان
392 nowhere ... ليس في أي مكان
393 loose ... محلول/ متراخي/مفكك
393 loosen ... يرخي
393 storm ... عاصفة
393 lightning ... برق
393 thunder ... رعد
393 blind ... أعمى
393 devil ... شيطان
394 ride ... يركب
394 cycle ... يركب دراجة
394 may ... أيمكن
394 can ... أيمكن
394 could ... أيمكن
394 permission ... إذن
394 catch ... يمسك بـ/يلتقط/يلحق بـ
394 raincoat ... معطف المطر
395 cap ... قبعة
395 habit ... عادة
395 be in the habit of doing ... من عادته أن يفعل
396 stranger ... الغريب
396 foreigner ... الأجنبي
396 snowstorm ... عاصفة ثلجية

LESSON 75

397 look like ... يشبه
397 travel ... سفر
397 journey ... رحلة
397 just ... فقط
398 of course ... بالطبع
398 nowadays ... في الوقت الحاضر
398 suffer ... يعاني من
398 wish ... أمنية
398 exist ... يوجد
399 remind ... يذكر
399 in other words ... أي
399 member ... فرد
399 library ... مكتبة
399 even though ... على الرغم من
399 even ... حتى
399 not even ... ولا حتى
400 to ... إلى
400 at ... عند
400 direction ... اتجاه
400 soon ... قريبًا
400 at once ... في الحال

LESSON 76

402 need ... يحتاج
402 towards ... نحو
402 destination ... وجهة
403 tray ... صينية
403 stadium ... مدرج
403 much better ... أفضل بكثير
403 much more ... أكثر من ذلك بكثير
403 contrary ... العكس
403 fall ... يسقط
403 temperature ... درجة الحرارة
403 atmosphere ... الغلاف الجوي
404 tooth ... سن
404 teeth ... أسنان
404 toothbrush ... فرشاة الأسنان
404 dentist ... طبيب الأسنان
404 seem ... يبدو
404 several ... بضع
405 compose ... يكون/يؤلف
405 be composed of ... يتكون من
405 wise ... من الحكمة
405 wisdom ... الحكمة
405 suddenly ... فجأة
405 pain ... ألم
406 certain ... متأكد
406 pass by ... يمر بجانب
406 park ... يركن
406 car park ... موقف السيارات
406 picture ... صورة

LESSON 77

409 diary ... مفكرة
410 character ... شخصية
410 really ... جدا
410 ran ... ركض
410 improve ... يحسن
410 coach ... مدرب
411 flew ... طار/قام برحلة جوية
411 wool ... صوف
412 apostrophe ... الفاصلة العليا
412 case ... حالة
412 kick ... يركل
413 coast ... الساحل
413 certain ... معين
413 tire ... يتعب/يمل

Chinese Vocabulary

LESSON 61

315 chat....................聊天
315 online....................在线
315 notice....................注意
315 free....................空闲；免费
315 busy....................忙碌
316 lie....................横放
316 comfortable....................舒服
316 uncomfortable....................不舒服
316 pillow....................枕头
316 wake up - woke up - woken up....................
.......醒来（过去式woke up；过去分词woken up)
316 go to sleep....................入睡
316 immediately....................立即
316 midnight....................午夜
317 through....................穿过
317 button....................纽扣
317 buttonhole....................纽扣孔
317 career....................职业生涯
317 cross....................十字架;表示错误的记号
317 crossroads....................十字路
317 test....................测试
318 danger....................危险
318 dangerous....................危险的（形容词)
318 dangerously....................危险地（副词)
318 alcohol....................酒精饮料
318 detective....................侦探
318 should....................应该
318 obligation....................义务
318 alternative....................选择
318 ambulance....................救护车
319 correct....................订正
319 grammatical....................语法的
319 problem....................问题
319 cause....................引起；原因
319 colleague....................同事
319 boss....................上司
319 freedom....................自由
319 justice....................正义
320 as....................因为
320 that is....................换言之，也就是说
320 bone....................骨头

LESSON 62

322 life....................生活
322 lives....................life的复数形式
322 the poor....................穷人们
322 the rich....................富人们
322 although....................虽然
322 cook....................烹饪
322 tasty....................好吃的
322 pasta....................意大利面
323 independent....................独立
323 origin....................起源
323 belong to....................属于
323 could.......can的过去式；也表示“可以，能”的意思
323 vice versa....................反之亦然
324 throw....................扔
324 alive....................活着的
324 dead....................死去的
324 drop....................让落下；落下；(一)滴
324 go without....................没有……也行
325 assassinate....................暗杀
325 usual....................经常
325 unusual....................不寻常
325 still....................依然
325 yet....................尚（未)，还（没)
325 in progress....................进行中
326 special....................特别的

LESSON 63

327 clean....................干净的
327 dirty....................肮脏的
327 dirt....................污垢
327 know of....................知道
327 to be afraid....................害怕
328 guard....................防范
328 on your guard....................警惕
328 off your guard....................放松警惕
328 calm....................使……平静；平静无风的（天气)
328 quietly....................轻声地
328 if I were....................如果我是……
328 king....................国王
328 person (1st, 2nd person etc.)....................
....................人称（第一人称、第二人称等等)
329 if I were you, ...如果我是你，……
329 advice....................建议
329 expression....................表达
329 especially....................尤其是
330 win - won - won....................胜利
....................(过去式won；过去分词won)
330 lottery....................彩票
330 useful....................有用的
330 useless....................没用的
330 possess....................拥有
331 take by surprise....................突袭

LESSON 64

332 contract....................缩小
333 sandwich....................三明治
333 cheese....................奶酪
333 fault....................错误
333 faultless....................无错误的
333 faulty....................有错误的
333 fix....................修理
334 OK....................好的，可以
334 all right....................好，行，可以
334 compare....................比较（动词)
334 comparison....................比较（名词)
334 have something in common....................有共通之处
334 ice....................冰
334 cool....................冷却
334 pour....................注入
335 unite....................结为一体
335 even....................甚至
335 surprising....................惊人的
335 mix....................混合
335 mixture....................混合物
335 pink....................粉红色
335 care....................照顾；介意
335 care for....................照料
335 take care of....................照顾
336 appointment....................约会
336 keep an appointment....................守约

336 hurry ....匆忙
336 take your time..慢慢来
336 plenty of...许多

LESSON 65

338 for ....表示持续一段时间
338 since ....自从
338 period ....期间
338 point...(时间)点
339 kitchen ....厨房
339 fridge ....冰箱
339 freezer ....冷冻库
339 cooker..炊具
339 sink..水槽
339 microwave ....微波炉
339 studies ....学习
340 lend - lent - lent 出借（过去式lent；过去分词lent)
340 return..归还
340 first name...名字，名
340 surname ....姓，姓氏
340 actor ....男演员
340 actress...女演员
340 famous...著名的
340 film star..电影演员
341 industrial ....工业的
341 agricultural...农业的
341 region ....地域
341 apologize..认错
341 apology..道歉
341 keep somebody waiting......................让某人等待
341 avoid...避免
341 bend ....弯腰
342 century..世纪
342 fashion...时尚
342 gate ....大门
342 worry...担心
342 be worried...担忧的
342 run ....跑

LESSON 66

344 I was speaking.. （过去进行时)我当时正在说……
344 particular..特定的
344 while ....当……的时候
345 earn ....赚
345 formal ....正式的
345 informal..非正式的
345 jeans..牛仔裤
345 trainer ....运动鞋
345 how do you do?.............. 你好（初次见面用语)
346 persuade ....说服
346 hairdresser ....理发师
346 so = very.............................. so = very（非常)
346 interesting...有趣的
346 exciting ....兴奋的
346 grammatically ....从语法上说
346 bathroom ....浴室
346 bath ....洗浴
346 shower..淋浴
346 toilet...厕所
346 basin ....洗脸台
347 mirror...镜子
347 reflect...反射
347 active ....主动式
347 passive ....被动式
347 subject..主语
347 object..宾语
348 by...被

LESSON 67

350 force ....强迫
350 make somebody do .... 使某人做某事
350 snack...零食
350 break ....休息时间
350 biscuit...饼干
350 crisps...薯片
350 to be born ....出生
351 murder...谋杀
351 prison..监狱
351 pupil...(小)学生
351 root ....根
351 memory ....记忆力
352 cross...穿过
353 think of...想起
353 safe...安全的
353 safety..安全
353 on your own ....独自
353 lay...平躺
354 sir...先生
354 madam ....女士
354 gentleman...绅士
354 lady ....女士，夫人，小姐
354 customer...顾客
354 officer...长官
354 title...称号，头衔
355 standard ....标准
355 height...身高
355 colourful ....色彩艳丽的

LESSON 68

356 would you say..
.................你会说……（询问别人意见时的问语)
356 opinion...看法
357 get in...进入
357 get out of ....出来
357 get on ....上车
357 get off ....下车
357 taxi...出租车
357 fare ....票价
357 royal..王室的
357 mud ....泥土
357 countryside ....乡村
357 crowd..人群
357 crowded ....拥挤的
358 captain...队长；船长
358 team ....团队
358 wide ....宽的
358 narrow ....窄的
358 flag...国旗
358 national...国家的
358 grass..草
358 live on .... 以……为食物
359 tower..塔；高楼
359 wet..湿的
359 dry ....干的
359 threw..throw的过去式
359 loud..大声的
359 turn up ....调大
359 turn down..调小
360 myself...我自己
360 yourself..你自己
360 himself...他自己
360 herself..她自己
360 itself..它自己
360 oneself...自己
360 ourselves..我们自己
360 yourselves ....你们自己

360 themselves ... 他们自己
360 consequently ... 结果，因此
360 protect ... 保护

LESSON 69

362 thorough ... 彻底的（形容词）
362 thoroughly ... 彻底地（副词）
362 accident ... 事故
362 by accident ... 偶然
363 careful ... 小心的
363 careless ... 不小心的
363 carefully ... 小心地
363 carelessly ... 不小心地;随意地
363 own ... 拥有
363 carry on ... 继续
363 retire ... 退休
364 prize ... 奖（金，品）
364 too ... 也，还
364 at least ... 至少
364 widely ... 广泛地
364 manner ... 举止；风格
364 pig ... 猪
365 asleep ... 睡着的
365 awake ... 醒着的
365 hospital ... 医院
365 nurse ... 护士
365 purpose ... 目的
365 in order to ... ... 为了
365 so that ... 以便，为了
365 take exercise ... 做运动
366 notice ... 通知
366 lain ... lie的过去分词
367 point at ... 指向
367 point out ... 指出
367 indicate ... 表明
367 grave ... 坟墓
368 neck ... 脖子
368 flame ... 火焰
368 flight ... 航程
368 soup ... 汤
368 except ... 除了

LESSON 70

369 may ... 可能
369 might ... may的过去式
369 palace ... 宫殿
369 parliament ... 议会
370 arrive at ... 到达（某一地点）
370 point ... 地点
370 arrive in ... 到达（某一地区）
370 area ... 地区
370 airport ... 机场
370 passport ... 护照
370 café ... 咖啡馆
370 owe ... 欠
370 souvenir ... 纪念品
371 pride ... 骄傲
371 proud ... 骄傲的
371 normal ... 通常
371 normally ... 通常地
371 take pride in ... 以……为骄傲
371 servant ... 佣人
372 wheel ... 轮子
372 lorry ... 卡车
372 arrow ... 箭
372 centimetre ... 厘米
372 metre ... 米
372 beard ... 胡子
372 true ... 真实的
372 false ... 错误的
372 paper (newspaper) ... 纸（报纸）
372 maintain ... 维持
373 it takes ... 需要
373 Ireland ... 爱尔兰
373 amount ... 数量
373 amount to ... 合计
373 further ... 更远的；额外的
373 Sweden ... 瑞典
373 in addition ... 另外
373 extra ... 额外的

LESSON 71

375 I had eaten ... （过去完成时)我已经吃了……
376 party ... 聚会；党派
376 political ... 政治的
377 mad ... 狂热的
377 crazy ... 生气的；疯狂的；有精神病的
377 UFO ... 不明飞行物
377 copy ... 抄袭；复制；副本
378 influence ... 影响
378 mouse ... 老鼠
378 mice ... mouse的复数
378 throat ... 喉咙
378 opportunity ... 机会
378 develop ... 发展
378 industry ... 工业
378 agriculture ... 农业
379 print ... 印刷
379 sand ... 沙子
379 beach ... 沙滩
379 desert ... 沙漠
379 bell ... 铃，钟
379 knock ... 敲
379 pay a visit ... 拜访
379 ring ... 按铃
379 shout ... 喊叫
380 stick ... 棍子
380 walking stick ... 拐杖
380 exclamation mark ... 感叹号

LESSON 72

381 reason ... 原因
381 illness ... 疾病
381 tiredness ... 疲劳
381 darkness ... 黑暗
381 alone ... 独自一人
382 already ... 已经
382 thrown ... throw的过去分词
382 in spite of ... 尽管
382 despite ... 尽管
383 anyone ... 任何人
383 someone ... 某人
383 no one (no-one) ... 没有人
384 borrow ... 借入
384 my own ... 我自己的
384 emphasize ... 强调
384 skin ... 皮肤
385 wire ... 电线；金属线
385 electricity ... 电
385 connection ... 连接
385 wireless ... 无线
385 Wi-Fi ... Wi-Fi无线网络
385 hyphen ... 连字符
385 boil ... 煮
385 fry ... 炸
385 roast ... 烤
385 brick ... 砖头
386 as well ... 同样，也

386 too .... 也，还
386 also .... 也，亦

LESSON 73

387 I will be speaking...... （将来进行时)我将会说……
387 inch .... 英寸
387 foot .... 英尺
387 yard .... 码
388 chain .... 链条
388 rise .... 升起，提高
388 constantly .... 总是，一直
389 belt .... 皮带
389 hourly .... 每小时地
389 daily .... 每天地
389 weekly .... 每周地
389 monthly .... 每月地
389 yearly .... 每年地
390 allow .... 允许
390 let – let – let .... 让（过去式let；过去分词let)
390 everyday .... 每一天

LESSON 74

392 anywhere .... 任何地方
392 somewhere .... 某个地方
392 not anywhere .... 任何地方都没有
392 nowhere .... 任何地方都不
393 loose .... 自由的，宽松的；零散的
393 loosen .... 解开
393 storm .... 暴风雨
393 lightning .... 闪电
393 thunder .... 雷
393 blind .... 瞎的
393 devil .... 魔鬼
394 ride .... 骑；乘坐
394 cycle .... 骑自行车
394 may .... 可以
394 can .... 能够
394 could .... 能，可以
394 permission .... 许可
394 catch .... 抓住；赶上；感染
394 raincoat .... 雨衣
395 cap .... 帽子
395 habit .... 习惯
395 be in the habit of doing .... 习惯做……
396 stranger .... 陌生人
396 foreigner .... 外国人
396 snowstorm .... 暴风雪

LESSON 75

397 look like .... 看起来像
397 travel .... 旅游
397 journey .... 旅行
397 just .... 只是，仅仅
398 of course .... 当然
398 nowadays .... 如今
398 suffer .... 遭受
398 wish .... 愿望
398 exist .... 存在
399 remind .... 提醒;使记起
399 in other words .... 换句话说
399 member .... 成员
399 library .... 图书馆
399 even though .... 即使
399 even .... 甚至；更
399 not even .... 甚至不
400 to .... 去
400 at .... 在
400 direction .... 方向
400 soon .... 很快
400 at once .... 立刻

LESSON 76

402 need .... 需要
402 towards .... 朝向
402 destination .... 目的地
403 tray .... 托盘
403 stadium .... 体育场
403 much better .... 好得多
403 much more .... 多得多
403 contrary .... 相反的事物
403 fall .... 下降
403 temperature .... 温度
403 atmosphere .... 大气
404 tooth .... 牙齿
404 teeth .... tooth的复数
404 toothbrush .... 牙刷
404 dentist .... 牙医
404 seem .... 似乎
404 several .... 若干，几个
405 compose .... 创作
405 be composed of .... 由……组成
405 wise .... 有智慧的
405 wisdom .... 智慧
405 suddenly .... 突然
405 pain .... 疼痛
406 certain .... 肯定的
406 pass by .... 经过
406 park .... 停车
406 car park .... 停车场
406 picture .... 描绘

LESSON 77

409 diary .... 日记
410 character .... 性格
410 really .... 真地，确实
410 ran .... run的过去式
410 improve .... 提高
410 coach .... 教练；长途旅行汽车
411 flew .... fly的过去式
411 wool .... 羊毛
412 apostrophe .... 撇号（'），所有格符号
412 case .... 格
412 kick .... 踢
413 coast .... 海岸
413 certain .... 某些，某个
413 tire .... 厌倦

Czech Vocabulary

LESSON 61

315 chat.......chat/chatovat
315 online.......online (připojen)
315 notice.......všimnout si
315 free.......volný/zdarma/bezplatný
315 busy.......zaneprázdněn
316 lie.......ležet
316 comfortable.......pohodlný
316 uncomfortable.......nepohodlný
316 pillow.......polštář
316 wake up - woke up - woken up.......vzbudit se: přítomný čas - minulý čas - příčestí minulé
316 go to sleep.......jít spát
316 immediately.......ihned
316 midnight.......půlnoc
317 through.......skrze
317 button.......knoflík
317 buttonhole.......knoflíková dírka
317 career.......profesní dráha/kariéra
317 cross.......křížek
317 crossroads.......křižovatka
317 test.......test
318 danger.......nebezpečí
318 dangerous.......nebezpečný
318 dangerously.......nebezpečně
318 alcohol.......alkohol
318 detective.......detektiv
318 should.......měl by
318 obligation.......povinnost
318 alternative.......jiná možnost/alternativa
318 ambulance.......sanitní vůz
319 correct.......opravit
319 grammatical.......gramatický
319 problem.......problém
319 cause.......způsobit/příčina
319 colleague.......spolupracovník
319 boss.......šéf
319 freedom.......svoboda
319 justice.......spravedlnost
320 as.......protože/jelikož
320 that is.......respektive/a sice/tedy
320 bone.......kost

LESSON 62

322 life.......život
322 lives.......životy
322 the poor.......chudý člověk
322 the rich.......bohatý člověk
322 although.......ačkoli
322 cook.......vařit/kuchař
322 tasty.......chutný
322 pasta.......těstoviny
323 independent.......nezávislý
323 origin.......původ
323 belong to.......patřit
323 couldminulý čas nebo podmiň. zp. od slovesa can (umět/moci)
323 vice versa.......obráceně/naopak
324 throw.......hodit
324 alive.......živý/nažlvu
324 dead.......mrtvý
324 drop.......upustit/padat/kapka
324 go without.......obejít se
325 assassinate.......spáchat atentát
325 usual.......obvyklý
325 unusual.......neobvyklý
325 still.......dosud/stále
325 yet.......ještě (ne)
325 in progress.......probíhat/trvající
326 special.......speciální/mimořádný

LESSON 63

327 clean.......čistý
327 dirty.......znečištěný
327 dirt.......špína
327 know of.......znát
327 to be afraid.......bát se
328 guard.......ochránit se
328 on your guard.......dávat si pozor
328 off your guard.......nedávat si pozor
328 calm.......tichý/uklidnit
328 quietly.......tiše
328 if I were.......kdybych byl ...
328 king.......král
328 person (1st, 2nd person etc.) . osoba (1., 2 osoba atd.)
329 if I were you, ...kdybych byl tebou ...
329 advice.......rada
329 expression.......výraz
329 especially.......zvláště/především
330 win - won - won ......vyhrát: přítomný čas - minulý čas - příčestí minulé
330 lottery.......loterie
330 useful.......užitečný
330 useless.......neužitečný
330 possess.......vlastnit/mít
331 take by surprise.......nechat se překvapit

LESSON 64

332 contract.......stáhnout
333 sandwich.......sendvič
333 cheese.......sýr
333 fault.......chyba
333 faultless.......bezchybný
333 faulty.......poruchový
333 fix.......napravit
334 OK.......OK
334 all right.......v pořádku
334 compare.......porovnat
334 comparison.......porovnání
334 have something in common mít něco společného
334 ice.......led
334 cool.......chladit
334 pour.......lít
335 unite.......sjednotit/spojit
335 even.......dokonce
335 surprising.......překvapivý
335 mix.......smíchat
335 mixture.......směs
335 pink.......růžová
335 care.......dbát/péče/záležet na něčem
335 care for.......pečovat o
335 take care of.......starat se o
336 appointment.......schůzka/setkání

336 keep an appointment dostavit se včas na schůzku
336 hurry ... spěchat
336 take your time ... dát si načas
336 plenty of ... spousta

LESSON 65

338 for ... po dobu (nepřekládá se)
338 since ... od
338 period ... období
338 point ... bod/okamžik
339 kitchen ... kuchyň
339 fridge ... lednička
339 freezer ... mraznička
339 cooker ... sporák
339 sink ... dřez
339 microwave ... mikrovlnná trouba
339 studies ... studia
340 lend - lent - lent ... půjčit - min. čas - příčestí min.
340 return ... vrátit
340 first name ... jméno
340 surname ... příjmení
340 actor ... herec
340 actress ... herečka
340 famous ... populární
340 film star ... filmová hvězda
341 industrial ... průmyslový
341 agricultural ... zemědělský
341 region ... oblast
341 apologize ... omluvit se
341 apology ... omluva
341 keep somebody waiting ... nechat někoho čekat
341 avoid ... vyhnout se
341 bend ... sehnout se/sklonit
342 century ... století
342 fashion ... móda
342 gate ... brána
342 worry ... strachovat se/obávat se
342 be worried ... mít strach/starost
342 run ... běžet

LESSON 66

344 I was speaking ... hovořil jsem
344 particular ... konkrétní/určitý
344 while ... zatímco
345 earn ... vydělat si
345 formal ... formální
345 informal ... neformální
345 jeans ... džíny
345 trainer ... teniska
345 how do you do? ... jak se máte? (pozdrav)
346 persuade ... přesvědčit
346 hairdresser ... kadeřník
346 so = very ... tak
346 interesting ... zajímavý
346 exciting ... vzrušující
346 grammatically ... gramaticky
346 bathroom ... koupelna
346 bath ... vana
346 shower ... sprcha
346 toilet ... WC
346 basin ... umyvadlo
347 mirror ... zrcadlo
347 reflect ... odrážet
347 active ... aktivní/činný
347 passive ... pasivní/trpný
347 subject ... podmět
347 object ... předmět
348 by ... (kým/čím)

LESSON 67

350 force ... nutit
350 make somebody do ... přimět někoho k něčemu
350 snack ... svačina
350 break ... přestávka
350 biscuit ... sušenka/pečivo
350 crisps ... lupínky
350 to be born ... narodit se
351 murder ... vražda
351 prison ... věznice
351 pupil ... žák
351 root ... kořen
351 memory ... paměť
352 cross ... přejít/přeplout
353 think of ... myslet na
353 safe ... bezpečný
353 safety ... bezpečnost
353 on your own ... sám (bez pomoci)
353 lay ... ležet (min. č.)
354 sir ... pan
354 madam ... paní
354 gentleman ... pán
354 lady ... dáma
354 customer ... zákazník
354 officer ... důstojník/úřední osoba
354 title ... titul
355 standard ... úroveň/běžný/normální
355 height ... výška
355 colourful ... pestrý

LESSON 68

356 would you say ... řekl byste/podle vašeho názoru
356 opinion ... názor
357 get in ... nasednout do
357 get out of ... vysednout z
357 get on ... nastoupit do
357 get off ... vystoupit z
357 taxi ... taxi
357 fare ... jízdné
357 royal ... královský
357 mud ... bláto
357 countryside ... venkov/krajina
357 crowd ... dav
357 crowded ... přeplněný
358 captain ... kapitán
358 team ... tým
358 wide ... široký
358 narrow ... úzký
358 flag ... vlajka
358 national ... národní/státní
358 grass ... tráva
358 live on ... živit se čím
359 tower ... věž
359 wet ... mokrý
359 dry ... suchý
359 threw ... hodit (min. čas od throw)
359 loud ... hlasitý
359 turn up ... zesílit (zvuk)
359 turn down ... ztlumit (zvuk)
360 myself ... já sám/sebe
360 yourself ... ty sám/sebe
360 himself ... on sám/sebe
360 herself ... ona sama/sebe
360 itself ... ono samo/sebe
360 oneself ... někdo sám/sebe
360 ourselves ... my sami/sebe
360 yourselves ... vy sami/sebe
360 themselves ... oni sami/sebe

360 consequently ... následně/tudíž
360 protect ... chránit

LESSON 69

362 thorough ... důkladný
362 thoroughly ... důkladně/naprosto
362 accident ... nehoda
362 by accident ... náhodou
363 careful ... pozorný
363 careless ... nedbalý
363 carefully ... pozorně
363 carelessly ... nedbale
363 own ... vlastnit
363 carry on ... pokračovat v
363 retire ... jít do důchodu
364 prize ... cena
364 too ... také
364 at least ... nejméně
364 widely ... rozsáhle/běžně
364 manner ... způsoby/chování
364 pig ... prase
365 asleep ... spící
365 awake ... bdělý
365 hospital ... nemocnice
365 nurse ... zdravotní sestra
365 purpose ... účel
365 in order to ... aby...
365 so that ... aby
365 take exercise ... zacvičit si
366 notice ... oznámení
366 lain ... ležet (příčestí min.)
367 point at ... ukázat na
367 point out ... poukázat na
367 indicate ... označit
367 grave ... hrob
368 neck ... krk
368 flame ... plamen
368 flight ... let
368 soup ... polévka
368 except ... vyjma

LESSON 70

369 may ... snad/možná
369 might ... snad/možná (podmiň. způsob)
369 palace ... palác
369 parliament ... parlament
370 arrive at ... dorazit k/na
370 point ... místo
370 arrive in ... dorazit do
370 area ... oblast
370 airport ... letiště
370 passport ... cestovní doklad
370 café ... kavárna
370 owe ... dlužit
370 souvenir ... suvenýr
371 pride ... pýcha/hrdost
371 proud ... hrdý
371 normal ... obvyklý
371 normally ... obvykle
371 take pride in ... být hrdý na
371 servant ... sluha
372 wheel ... kolo
372 lorry ... nákladní vozidlo
372 arrow ... šíp
372 centimetre ... centimetr
372 metre ... metr
372 beard ... vous
372 true ... správně/pravda
372 false ... nesprávně/nepravda
372 paper (newspaper) ... noviny
372 maintain ... udržovat
373 it takes ... trvá
373 Ireland ... Irsko
373 amount ... částka/množství
373 amount to ... činit/obnášet
373 further ... dále/další/dodatečný
373 Sweden ... Švédsko
373 in addition ... dodatečně/navíc
373 extra ... mimořádný/navíc

LESSON 71

375 I had eaten ... jedl/a jsem
376 party ... večírek/politická strana/skupina
376 political ... politický
377 mad ... zuřivý/šílený/blázen do
377 crazy ... bláznivý
377 UFO ... UFO
377 copy ... opisovat/opakovat/kopírovat/kopie
378 influence ... vliv
378 mouse ... myš
378 mice ... myši
378 throat ... hrdlo
378 opportunity ... příležitost
378 develop ... rozvíjet
378 industry ... průmysl
378 agriculture ... zemědělství
379 print ... tisknout
379 sand ... písek
379 beach ... pláž
379 desert ... poušť
379 bell ... zvonek
379 knock ... klepat
379 pay a visit ... navštívit
379 ring ... zvonit
379 shout ... křičet
380 stick ... hůl/klacek
380 walking stick ... vycházková hůl
380 exclamation mark ... vykřičník

LESSON 72

381 reason ... důvod
381 illness ... nemoc
381 tiredness ... únava
381 darkness ... temnota
381 alone ... samoten
382 already ... již
382 thrown ... hodit (příčestí minulé od throw)
382 in spite of ... navzdory/ačkoli
382 despite ... navzdory/ačkoli
383 anyone ... někdo (v tázací větě)
383 someone ... někdo (v oznamovací větě)
383 no one (no-one) ... nikdo
384 borrow ... půjčit si
384 my own ... můj vlastní
384 emphasize ... zdůraznit
384 skin ... pokožka/kůže
385 wire ... drát
385 electricity ... elektřina
385 connection ... zapojení
385 wireless ... bezdrátový
385 Wi-Fi ... Wi-Fi
385 hyphen ... pomlčka
385 boil ... vařit
385 fry ... smažit
385 roast ... opékat
385 brick ... cihla

386 as well .... také
386 too .... také
386 also .... také

LESSON 73

387 I will be speaking... budu hovořit (průběhový čas)
387 inch .... palec
387 foot .... stopa
387 yard .... yard
388 chain .... řetízek/řetězový
388 rise .... zvedat se/vstávat/růst
388 constantly .... trvale/stále
389 belt .... opasek
389 hourly .... každou hodinu
389 daily .... denně
389 weekly .... týdně
389 monthly .... měsíčně
389 yearly .... ročně
390 allow .... umožnit/dovolit/nechat
390 let – let – let .... nechat: přítomný čas - minulý čas - příčestí minulé
390 everyday .... každý den

LESSON 74

392 anywhere .... někde (v tázací větě)
392 somewhere .... někde (v oznamovací větě)
392 not anywhere .... nikde
392 nowhere .... nikde
393 loose .... volný, nepřivázaný, neupevněný
393 loosen .... uvolnit
393 storm .... bouře
393 lightning .... blesk
393 thunder .... hrom
393 blind .... slepý
393 devil .... ďábel
394 ride .... jet na
394 cycle .... jet na kole
394 may .... smět/být možné
394 can .... umět/moci
394 couldminulý čas nebo podmiň. zp. od slovesa can (umět/moci)
394 permission .... povolení
394 catch .... chytit/dostat
394 raincoat .... pláštěnka
395 cap .... pokrývka hlavy (např. proti slunci)
395 habit .... zvyk
395 be in the habit of doing .... mít ve zvyku
396 stranger .... cizí člověk
396 foreigner .... cizinec
396 snowstorm .... sněhová bouře

LESSON 75

397 look like .... vypadat jako
397 travel .... cestovat
397 journey .... cesta
397 just .... pouze
398 of course .... samozřejmě
398 nowadays .... v současnosti
398 suffer .... trpět
398 wish .... přání
398 exist .... existovat
399 remind .... připomenout/upomenout
399 in other words .... jinými slovy
399 member .... člen
399 library .... knihovna
399 even though .... dokonce i když
399 even .... dokonce
399 not even .... dokonce ani
400 to .... k/do
400 at .... u/při
400 direction .... směr
400 soon .... brzy
400 at once .... ihned

LESSON 76

402 need .... potřebovat
402 towards .... směrem k
402 destination .... cíl/destinace
403 tray .... tác
403 stadium .... stadion
403 much better .... mnohem lepší/lépe
403 much more .... mnohem více
403 contrary .... opak
403 fall .... klesnout
403 temperature .... teplota
403 atmosphere .... atmosféra
404 tooth .... zub
404 teeth .... zuby
404 toothbrush .... zubní kartáček
404 dentist .... zubař
404 seem .... zdát se/vypadat
404 several .... několik
405 compose .... složit/skládat
405 be composed of .... skládat se z
405 wise .... moudrý
405 wisdom .... moudrost
405 suddenly .... náhle
405 pain .... bolest
406 certain .... jistý
406 pass by .... míjet
406 park .... parkovat
406 car park .... parkoviště
406 picture .... zobrazovat

LESSON 77

409 diary .... deník
410 character .... charakter/povaha/osobnost
410 really .... skutečně
410 ran .... běžet (minulý čas slovesa run)
410 improve .... zlepšit/zdokonalit
410 coach .... trenér/autokar
411 flew .... letět (minulý čas slovesa fly)
411 wool .... vlna
412 apostrophe .... apostrof
412 case .... tvar/způsob
412 kick .... kopat
413 coast .... pobřeží
413 certain .... některý/určitý
413 tire .... unavit se

French Vocabulary

LESSON 61

315 chat.......chatter / bavarder
315 online.......en ligne
315 notice.......remarquer
315 free.......libre / gratuit
315 busy.......occupé
316 lie.......être posé / être couché
316 comfortable.......confortable
316 uncomfortable.......inconfortable
316 pillow.......coussin / oreiller
316 wake up - woke up - woken up.......se réveiller
316 go to sleep.......s'endormir
316 immediately.......immédiatement
316 midnight.......minuit
317 through.......via / par / à travers
317 button.......bouton
317 buttonhole.......boutonnière
317 career.......carrière
317 cross.......croix
317 crossroads.......croisement
317 test.......test / contrôle
318 danger.......danger
318 dangerous.......dangereux
318 dangerously.......dangereusement
318 alcohol.......alcool
318 detective.......détective
318 should.......je devrais / tu devrais / il devrais / .... nous devrions / vous devriez / ils devraient
318 obligation.......obligation
318 alternative.......alternative / autre option / .... autre choix / autre possibilité
318 ambulance.......ambulance
319 correct.......corriger
319 grammatical.......grammatical
319 problem.......problème
319 cause.......causer / cause
319 colleague.......collègue
319 boss.......patron
319 freedom.......liberté
319 justice.......justice
320 as.......puisque / comme
320 that is.......disons / c'est-à-dire
320 bone.......os

LESSON 62

322 life.......vie
322 lives.......vies
322 the poor.......les pauvres
322 the rich.......les riches
322 although.......même si / bien que / quoique
322 cook.....cuisiner / cuisinier / cuisinière (personne)
322 tasty.......savoureux
322 pasta.......pâtes
323 independent.......indépendant
323 origin.......origine
323 belong to.......appartenir à
323 could.......passé et conditionnel de pouvoir
323 vice versa.......vice versa
324 throw.......jeter
324 alive.......vivant
324 dead.......mort
324 drop.......laisser tomber / tomber / goutte
324 go without se priver de / faire sans / se passer de
325 assassinate.......assassiner
325 usual.......habituel
325 unusual.......inhabituel
325 still.......encore / toujours
325 yet.......encore / déjà
325 in progress.......en progression / en cours
326 special.......spécial / particulier

LESSON 63

327 clean.......propre
327 dirty.......sale
327 dirt.......saleté / boue
327 know of.......connaître / être au courant de / ....entendre parler
327 to be afraid.......avoir peur
328 guard.......se protéger
328 on your guard.......sur ses gardes
328 off your guard.......ne pas être sur ses gardes
328 calm.......calmer / calme
328 quietly.......calmement
328 if I were.......si j'étais...
328 king.......roi
328 person (1st, 2nd person etc.).......personne ....(1ère, 2ème personne, etc)
329 if I were you, ...si j'étais à ta/votre place, ...
329 advice.......conseil
329 expression.......expression
329 especially... spécialement / surtout / en particulier
330 win - won - won.......gagner
330 lottery.......loterie
330 useful.......utile
330 useless.......inutile
330 possess.......posséder
331 take by surprise.......prendre par surprise

LESSON 64

332 contract.......contracter
333 sandwich.......sandwich
333 cheese.......fromage
333 fault.......défaut / anomalie / faute
333 faultless.......parfait / irréprochable
333 faulty.......défectueux
333 fix.......corriger / réparer
334 OK.......OK
334 all right.......très bien / d'accord
334 compare.......comparer
334 comparison.......comparaison
334 have something in common.......avoir quelque ....chose en commun
334 ice.......glace / glaçon
334 cool.......refroidir / rafraîchir
334 pour.......verser
335 unite.......s'unir
335 even.......même
335 surprising.......surprenant
335 mix.......mélanger
335 mixture.......mélange
335 pink.......rose
335 care.......se soucier / s'intéresser
335 care for.......s'occuper de
335 take care of.......prendre soin de

336 appointment.................................... rendez-vous
336 keep an appointment se rendre à un rendez-vous
336 hurry .... se dépêcher
336 take your time....................... prenez votre temps
336 plenty of....................... largement / bien assez de

LESSON 65

338 for .... depuis
338 since .... depuis
338 period .... période
338 point.. point / moment
339 kitchen .... cuisine
339 fridge .... réfrigérateur
339 freezer .... congélateur
339 cooker.. cuisinière
339 sink .... évier
339 microwave .... four à micro-ondes
339 studies .... études
340 lend - lent - lent.. prêter
340 return .... rendre
340 first name.. prénom
340 surname .... nom de famille / patronyme
340 actor .... acteur
340 actress .... actrice
340 famous.. célèbre
340 film star......................... star / vedette de cinéma
341 industrial .... industriel
341 agricultural... agricole
341 region .... région
341 apologize ...... s'excuser / présenter ses excuses / .... demander pardon
341 apology .... excuse
341 keep somebody waiting.. faire attendre quelqu'un
341 avoid .... éviter
341 bend .... se pencher
342 century .... siècle
342 fashion .... mode
342 gate .... portail
342 worry .... s'inquiéter
342 be worried.. être inquiet
342 run .... courir

LESSON 66

344 I was speaking................. j'étais en train de parler
344 particular .... particulier
344 while .... pendant que / alors que
345 earn .... gagner (de l'argent)
345 formal .... formel
345 informal.. informel
345 jeans .... jean
345 trainer .... tennis / chaussure de sport
345 how do you do?. ravi de faire votre connaissance
346 persuade .... persuader
346 hairdresser .... coiffeur / coiffeuse
346 so = very .... tellement / tant
346 interesting .... intéressant
346 exciting .... passionnant
346 grammatically .... grammaticalement
346 bathroom .... salle de bains
346 bath .... bain
346 shower .... douche
346 toilet .... toilettes
346 basin .... lavabo
347 mirror .... miroir
347 reflect .... refléter
347 active .... actif
347 passive .... passif
347 subject .... sujet
347 object .... objet
348 by... par

LESSON 67

350 force .... forcer / obliger
350 make somebody do ... . faire faire quelque .... chose à quelqu'un
350 snack .... encas / snack
350 break .... pause
350 biscuit .... biscuit
350 crisps .... chips
350 to be born .... être né
351 murder .... meurtre
351 prison .... prison
351 pupil .... élève
351 root .... racine
351 memory .... mémoire
352 cross .... traverser
353 think of.. penser à
353 safe... sûr / sans danger
353 safety .... sécurité
353 on your own .... tout seul
353 lay .... passé du verbe "lie"
354 sir.. monsieur / chef / .... rang militaire ....(par ex. sergent, capitaine, commandant, etc.)
354 madam .... madame
354 gentleman.............................. homme / monsieur
354 lady .... femme / dame
354 customer .... client
354 officer .... officier
354 title .... titre
355 standard .... niveau / standard / norme
355 height.. taille / hauteur
355 colourful .... coloré

LESSON 68

356 would you say.................................... diriez-vous
356 opinion .... opinion / avis
357 get in... monter (dans)
357 get out of .... sortir de / descendre de
357 get on .... monter (dans)
357 get off .... sortir (de) / descendre (de)
357 taxi .... taxi
357 fare .... ticket/billet
357 royal... royal
357 mud .... boue
357 countryside .... campagne
357 crowd .... foule
357 crowded .... bondé
358 captain .... capitaine
358 team .... équipe
358 wide .... large
358 narrow .... étroit
358 flag .... drapeau
358 national .... national
358 grass .... herbe
358 live on .... se nourrir de
359 tower .... tour
359 wet .... mouillé
359 dry .... sec
359 threw.............................. passé du verbe "throw"
359 loud.. fort / sonore
359 turn up ...mettre plus fort / monter le son / volume
359 turn down............................... mettre moins fort / .... baisser le son / volume
360 myself .... me
360 yourself .... te
360 himself .... se
360 herself.. se

360 itself ... se
360 oneself ... se
360 ourselves ... nous
360 yourselves ... vous
360 themselves ... se
360 consequently ... par conséquent
360 protect ... protéger

LESSON 69

362 thorough ... complet
362 thoroughly ... complètement
362 accident ... accident
362 by accident ... par accident
363 careful ... prudent / soigneux
363 careless ... imprudent / négligé
363 carefully ... prudemment
363 carelessly ... négligemment
363 own ... posséder / être propriétaire (de)
363 carry on ... continuer / poursuivre
363 retire ... prendre sa retraite
364 prize ... prix
364 too ... également
364 at least ... au moins
364 widely ... couramment
364 manner ... manière
364 pig ... cochon
365 asleep ... endormi
365 awake ... (r)éveillé
365 hospital ... hôpital
365 nurse ... infirmier / infirmière
365 purpose ... intention / finalité
365 in order to ... ... afin de / pour
365 so that ... pour que / afin que
365 take exercise ... faire de l'exercice
366 notice ... affiche
366 lain ... allongé / couché
367 point at ... pointer (du doigt)
367 point out ... indiquer / mentionner
367 indicate ... indiquer
367 grave ... tombe
368 neck ... cou
368 flame ... flamme
368 flight ... vol
368 soup ... soupe
368 except ... excepté / sauf

LESSON 70

369 may ... il se peut que
369 might ... conditionnel de may = il se pourrait que
369 palace ... palais
369 parliament ... parlement
370 arrive at ... arriver à / parvenir à
370 point ... point
370 arrive in ... arriver à / en / dans
370 area ... zone / région
370 airport ... aéroport
370 passport ... passeport
370 café ... café
370 owe ... devoir (de l'argent ou quelque chose)
370 souvenir ... souvenir
371 pride ... fierté
371 proud ... fier
371 normal ... normal
371 normally ... normalement
371 take pride in ... être fier de
371 servant ... domestique
372 wheel ... roue
372 lorry ... camion
372 arrow ... flèche
372 centimetre ... centimètre
372 metre ... mètre
372 beard ... barbe
372 true ... vrai
372 false ... faux
372 paper (newspaper) ... journal
372 maintain ... entretenir
373 it takes ... il faut / cela prend
373 Ireland ... Irlande
373 amount ... montant / quantité
373 amount to ... s'élever à / équivaloir à / ... égaler / représenter / correspondre à
373 further ... plus loin / davantage
373 Sweden ... Suède
373 in addition ... de / en plus / en supplément
373 extra ... supplémentaire

LESSON 71

375 I had eaten ... j'avais mangé
376 party ... parti / fête / groupe
376 political ... politique
377 mad ... fou
377 crazy ... fou / dingue
377 UFO ... OVNI
377 copy ... copier / copie
378 influence ... influence
378 mouse ... souris (sing.)
378 mice ... souris (pl.)
378 throat ... gorge
378 opportunity ... opportunité / occasion
378 develop ... développer
378 industry ... industrie
378 agriculture ... agriculture
379 print ... imprimer
379 sand ... sable
379 beach ... plage
379 desert ... désert
379 bell ... sonnerie
379 knock ... toquer / frapper
379 pay a visit ... rendre visite
379 ring ... sonner
379 shout ... crier
380 stick ... bâton
380 walking stick ... canne
380 exclamation mark ... point d'exclamation

LESSON 72

381 reason ... raison
381 illness ... maladie
381 tiredness ... fatigue
381 darkness ... obscurité
381 alone ... seul
382 already ... déjà
382 thrown ... jeté
382 in spite of ... malgré / en dépit de
382 despite ... malgré / en dépit de
383 anyone ... quelqu'un / n'importe qui
383 someone ... quelqu'un
383 no one (no-one) ... personne
384 borrow ... emprunter
384 my own ... mon/ma propre + noun / ... le mien / la mienne / ... les miens / les miennes
384 emphasize ... insister sur le fait que / souligner
384 skin ... peau
385 wire ... câble
385 electricity ... électricité
385 connection ... connexion
385 wireless ... sans fil

385 Wi-Fi ... Wifi
385 hyphen ... trait d'union
385 boil ... (faire) bouilllr
385 fry ... (faire) frire
385 roast ... (faire) rôtir
385 brick ... brique
386 as well ... également / aussi
386 too ... également / aussi
386 also ... également / aussi

LESSON 73

387 I will be speaking ... je serai en train de parler
387 inch ... pouce
387 foot ... pied
387 yard ... yard
388 chain ... chaîne
388 rise ... s'élever / se lever / augmenter
388 constantly ... constamment / sans cesse
389 belt ... ceinture
389 hourly ... toutes les heures
389 daily ... quotidien(-nement) / tous les jours
389 weekly ... hebdomadaire(-ment) / ... toutes les semaines
389 monthly ... mensuel(-lement) / tous les mois
389 yearly ... annuel(-lement) / tous les ans
390 allow ... permettre
390 let – let – let ... permettre / laisser
390 everyday ... de tous les jours / quotidien

LESSON 74

392 anywhere ... quelque part / n'importe où
392 somewhere ... quelque part
392 not anywhere ... nulle part / pas n'importe où
392 nowhere ... nulle part
393 loose ... en liberté / flottant / branlant
393 loosen ... relâcher / détendre / défaire
393 storm ... tempête
393 lightning ... éclair
393 thunder ... tonnerre
393 blind ... aveugle
393 devil ... diable
394 ride ... monter (à)
394 cycle ... vélo
394 may ... pouvoir (ex.: may I? Puis-je ?)
394 can ... pouvoir
394 could. pouvoir in the past tense or the conditional
394 permission ... permission
394 catch ... attraper / prendre
394 raincoat ... imperméable
395 cap ... casquette
395 habit ... habitude
395 be in the habit of doing ... avoir l'habitude de faire
396 stranger ... étranger
396 foreigner ... étranger
396 snowstorm ... tempête de neige

LESSON 75

397 look like ... ressembler / on dirait que / ... cela m'a l'air d'être
397 travel ... voyager
397 journey ... voyage
397 just ... juste
398 of course ... bien sûr / évidemment
398 nowadays ... de nos jours
398 suffer ... souffrir
398 wish ... souhait
398 exist ... exister
399 remind ... rappeler
399 in other words ... en d'autres termes
399 member ... membre
399 library ... bibliothèque
399 even though ... quand bien même / même si
399 even ... même / encore
399 not even ... même pas
400 to ... à
400 at ... à
400 direction ... direction
400 soon ... bientôt
400 at once ... immédiatement / tout de suite

LESSON 76

402 need ... avoir besoin de
402 towards ... vers
402 destination ... destination
403 tray ... plateau
403 stadium ... stade
403 much better ... bien mieux, bien meilleur
403 much more ... bien plus
403 contrary ... contraire
403 fall ... chuter / tomber
403 temperature ... température
403 atmosphere ... atmosphère
404 tooth ... dent
404 teeth ... dents
404 toothbrush ... brosse à dents
404 dentist ... dentiste
404 seem ... sembler
404 several ... plusieurs
405 compose ... composer
405 be composed of ... être composé de / ... se composer de
405 wise ... judicieux / sage
405 wisdom ... sagesse
405 suddenly ... soudain
405 pain ... douleur
406 certain ... certain / sûr
406 pass by ... passer / défiler
406 park ... garer
406 car park ... parking
406 picture ... s'imaginer / se représenter

LESSON 77

409 diary ... agenda
410 character ... caractère
410 really ... vraiment / très
410 ran ... passé du verbe "run"
410 improve ... améliorer
410 coach ... entraîneur / car
411 flew ... passé du verbe "fly"
411 wool ... laine
412 apostrophe ... apostrophe
412 case ... cas
412 kick ... donner un coup de pied
413 coast ... côte
413 certain ... certain
413 tire ... se lasser de

German Vocabulary

LESSON 61

315 chat ... plaudern
315 online ... online
315 notice ... bemerken
315 free ... frei haben / kostenlos / umsonst
315 busy ... beschäftigt
316 lie ... liegen
316 comfortable ... bequem
316 uncomfortable ... unbequem
316 pillow ... Kissen
316 wake up - woke up - woken up ... aufwachen
316 go to sleep ... schlafen gehen
316 immediately ... sofort
316 midnight ... Mitternacht
317 through ... durch
317 button ... Knopf
317 buttonhole ... Knopfloch
317 career ... Laufbahn
317 cross ... Kreuz
317 crossroads ... Kreuzung
317 test ... Test
318 danger ... Gefahr
318 dangerous ... gefährlich
318 dangerously ... gefährlich
318 alcohol ... Alkohol
318 detective ... Detektiv
318 should ... sollte
318 obligation ... Verpflichtung
318 alternative ... Alternative
318 ambulance ... Krankenwagen
319 correct ... korrekt
319 grammatical ... grammatikalisch
319 problem ... Problem
319 cause ... verursachen / Grund
319 colleague ... Kollege
319 boss ... Chef
319 freedom ... Freiheit
319 justice ... Gerechtigkeit
320 as ... da / als / wie
320 that is ... das heißt
320 bone ... Knochen

LESSON 62

322 life ... Leben (Singular)
322 lives ... Leben (Plural)
322 the poor ... die Armen
322 the rich ... die Reichen
322 although ... obwohl
322 cook ... kochen / Koch
322 tasty ... lecker
322 pasta ... Pasta
323 independent ... unabhängig
323 origin ... Ursprung
323 belong to ... gehören
323 could ... könnte
323 vice versa ... umgekehrt
324 throw ... werfen
324 alive ... am Leben
324 dead ... tot
324 drop ... fallen lassen / Tropfen
324 go without ... ohne etwas auskommen
325 assassinate ... ermorden
325 usual ... normal
325 unusual ... ungewöhnlich
325 still ... noch
325 yet ... noch nicht
325 in progress ... im Gang
326 special ... besonders

LESSON 63

327 clean ... sauber
327 dirty ... schmutzig
327 dirt ... Schmutz
327 know of ... kennen
327 to be afraid ... Angst haben
328 guard ... sich schützen
328 on your guard ... wachsam
328 off your guard ... unachtsam
328 calm ... beruhigen/ruhig
328 quietly ... ruhig
328 if I were ... wenn ich … wäre
328 king ... König
328 person (1st, 2nd person etc.) ... Person ... (1. Person, 2. Person etc.)
329 if I were you, ... wenn ich du/Sie wäre, …
329 advice ... Rat
329 expression ... Ausdruck
329 especially ... besonders
330 win - won - won ... gewinnen
330 lottery ... Lotterie
330 useful ... nützlich
330 useless ... nutzlos
330 possess ... besitzen
331 take by surprise ... überraschen

LESSON 64

332 contract ... zusammenziehen
333 sandwich ... Sandwich
333 cheese ... Käse
333 fault ... Fehler / Charakterschwäche
333 faultless ... fehlerfrei
333 faulty ... defekt
333 fix ... beheben
334 OK ... OK
334 all right ... in Ordnung
334 compare ... vergleichen
334 comparison ... Vergleich
334 have something in common ... etwas gemeinsam haben
334 ice ... Eis
334 cool ... kühl
334 pour ... gießen
335 unite ... vereinigen
335 even ... sogar
335 surprising ... überraschend
335 mix ... mischen
335 mixture ... Mischung
335 pink ... rosa / pink
335 care ... sorgen
335 care for ... sorgen für
335 take care of ... sich kümmern um
336 appointment ... Termin
336 keep an appointment ... einen Termin einhalten
336 hurry ... sich beeilen

336 take your time.............................. sich Zeit lassen
336 plenty of..viel

LESSON 65

338 for .... seit / für
338 since.. seit
338 period ....Zeitraum
338 point.. Zeitpunkt
339 kitchen ....Küche
339 fridge .... Kühlschrank
339 freezer .... Gefrierschrank
339 cooker... Herd
339 sink..Spüle
339 microwave .... Mikrowelle
339 studies ....Studium
340 lend - lent - lent..........................leihen / verleihen
340 return .... zurückgeben
340 first name... Vorname
340 surname ....Nachname
340 actor .... Schauspieler
340 actress.. Schauspielerin
340 famous..berühmt
340 film star... Filmstar
341 industrial ....industriell
341 agricultural................................landwirtschaftlich
341 region ....Region
341 apologize......................................entschuldigen
341 apology.................................... Entschuldigung
341 keep somebody waiting........... jemanden warten
....lassen
341 avoid.. vermeiden
341 bend ....bücken / Kurve
342 century..Jahrhundert
342 fashion..Mode
342 gate ....Tor
342 worry................................... sich Sorgen machen
342 be worried.. besorgt sein
342 run ....rennen

LESSON 66

344 I was speaking.....................Ich sprach (gerade) /
............................ich habe (gerade) gesprochen
344 particular... bestimmt
344 while .... während
345 earn .... verdienen
345 formal .... förmlich
345 informal... informell
345 jeans... Jeans
345 trainer ....Turnschuh
345 how do you do?..............wie geht es Ihnen / dir?
346 persuade ....überzeugen
346 hairdresser ....Friseur
346 so = very...so = sehr
346 interesting....................................... interessant
346 exciting .... spannend
346 grammatically ....grammatikalisch
346 bathroom ....Bad
346 bath .... Badewanne
346 shower...Dusche
346 toilet... Toilette
346 basin... Waschbecken
347 mirror ....Spiegel
347 reflect... reflektieren
347 active ....aktiv
347 passive ....passiv
347 subject...Subjekt
347 object..Objekt
348 by.. von

LESSON 67

350 force ....zwingen
350 make somebody do .....jemanden zwingen etwas
....zu tun ...
350 snack .... Snack
350 break ....Pause
350 biscuit ....Keks
350 crisps..Chips
350 to be born .... geboren sein
351 murder ....Mord
351 prison...Gefängnis
351 pupil...Schüler
351 root ....Wurzeln
351 memory ....Gedächtnis
352 cross ....überqueren
353 think of... denken an
353 safe.. sicher
353 safety .... Sicherheit
353 on your own...allein
353 lay.. lag
354 sir...mein Herr
354 madam ....meine Dame
354 gentleman..Herr
354 lady .... Dame
354 customer...Kunde
354 officer...Offizier
354 title... Titel / Anrede
355 standard .... Standard
355 height.. Größe / Höhe
355 colourful ....farbenfroh

LESSON 68

356 would you say......würdest du / würden Sie sagen
356 opinion .... Meinung
357 get in..einsteigen
357 get out of ....aussteigen
357 get on ....einsteigen
357 get off ....aussteigen
357 taxi... Taxi
357 fare ....Fahrpreis
357 royal...königlich
357 mud .... Matsch
357 countryside............................Natur / Landschaft
357 crowd... Menschenmasse
357 crowded..voll
358 captain..Kapitän
358 team ....Team
358 wide ....breit
358 narrow ....schmal
358 flag..Flagge
358 national..Landes-
358 grass.. Gras
358 live on .... leben von
359 tower..Turm
359 wet... nass
359 dry .... trocken
359 threw...................................... warf / werfen würde
359 loud.. laut
359 turn up ....lauter stellen
359 turn down.. leiser stellen
360 myself.........................mich (selbst) / mir (selbst)
360 yourself.......dich / sich (selbst) / dir / sich (selbst)
360 himself..sich (selbst)
360 herself...sich (selbst)
360 itself..sich (selbst)
360 oneself..sich (selbst)
360 ourselves ....uns (selbst)
360 yourselves ....euch (selbst)

German vocabulary

360 themselves .... sich (selbst)
360 consequently .... folglich
360 protect .... schützen

LESSON 69

362 thorough .... gründlich
362 thoroughly .... völlig
362 accident .... Unfall
362 by accident .... aus Versehen
363 careful .... vorsichtig
363 careless .... unvorsichtig
363 carefully .... sorgfältig
363 carelessly .... nachlässig
363 own .... besitzen
363 carry on .... etwas weiter tun
363 retire .... in den Ruhestand gehen
364 prize .... Preis
364 too .... auch
364 at least .... mindestens
364 widely .... häufig
364 manner .... Manieren/Art und Weise
364 pig .... Schwein
365 asleep .... schlafen
365 awake .... wach
365 hospital .... Krankenhaus
365 nurse .... Krankenschwester
365 purpose .... Zweck
365 in order to ... . um zu ...
365 so that .... damit
365 take exercise .... Sport treiben
366 notice .... Aushang
366 lain .... gelegen
367 point at .... zeigen auf
367 point out .... betonen
367 indicate .... anzeigen
367 grave .... Grab
368 neck .... Nacken
368 flame .... Flamme
368 flight .... Flug
368 soup .... Suppe
368 except .... außer

LESSON 70

369 may .... etw. vielleicht tun
369 might .... etw. vielleicht tun
369 palace .... Palast
369 parliament .... Parlament
370 arrive at .... ankommen an
370 point .... Punkt
370 arrive in .... ankommen in
370 area .... Gebiet
370 airport .... Flughafen
370 passport .... Pass
370 café .... Café
370 owe .... schulden
370 souvenir .... Souvenir
371 pride .... Stolz
371 proud .... stolz
371 normal .... normal
371 normally .... normalerweise
371 take pride in .... auf etw. stolz sein
371 servant .... Bediensteter / Bedienstete
372 wheel .... Rad
372 lorry .... Lastwagen
372 arrow .... Pfeil
372 centimetre .... Zentimeter
372 metre .... Meter
372 beard .... Bart
372 true .... wahr
372 false .... falsch
372 paper (newspaper) .... Zeitung
372 maintain .... unterhalten
373 it takes .... es dauert / ich brauche
373 Ireland .... Irland
373 amount .... Betrag / Menge
373 amount to .... ergeben
373 further .... weiter entfernt / weiteres / weitere
373 Sweden .... Schweden
373 in addition .... außerdem
373 extra .... zusätzlich

LESSON 71

375 I had eaten .... Ich hatte gegessen
376 party .... Partei/Party/Gruppe
376 political .... politisch
377 mad .... verärgert / begeistert / verrückt
377 crazy .... verrückt
377 UFO .... UFO
377 copy .... abschreiben/Ausgabe
378 influence .... Einfluss
378 mouse .... Maus
378 mice .... Mäuse
378 throat .... Hals
378 opportunity .... Möglichkeit
378 develop .... entwickeln
378 industry .... Industrie
378 agriculture .... Landwirtschaft
379 print .... drucken
379 sand .... Sand
379 beach .... Strand
379 desert .... Wüste
379 bell .... Klingel
379 knock .... klopfen
379 pay a visit .... besuchen
379 ring .... klingeln
379 shout .... schreien
380 stick .... Stock
380 walking stick .... Gehstock
380 exclamation mark .... Ausrufezeichen

LESSON 72

381 reason .... Grund
381 illness .... Krankheit
381 tiredness .... Müdigkeit
381 darkness .... Dunkelheit
381 alone .... allein
382 already .... bereits
382 thrown .... geworfen
382 in spite of .... trotz
382 despite .... trotz
383 anyone .... irgendjemand
383 someone .... jemand
383 no one (no-one) .... keiner / keine
384 borrow .... leihen / ausleihen
384 my own .... mein eigener / eigene / eigenes
384 emphasize .... betonen
384 skin .... Haut
385 wire .... Kabel
385 electricity .... Elektrizität
385 connection .... Verbindung
385 wireless .... drahtlos
385 Wi-Fi .... WLAN
385 hyphen .... Bindestrich
385 boil .... kochen
385 fry .... braten
385 roast .... rösten
385 brick .... Ziegel
386 as well .... auch

386 too ... auch
386 also ... auch

LESSON 73

387 I will be speaking ... Ich werde sprechen
387 inch ... Zoll
387 foot ... Fuß
387 yard ... Yard
388 chain ... Kette
388 rise ... aufsteigen / aufgehen / ansteigen
388 constantly ... ständig
389 belt ... Gürtel
389 hourly ... stündlich
389 daily ... täglich
389 weekly ... wöchentlich
389 monthly ... monatlich
389 yearly ... jährlich
390 allow ... lassen
390 let - let - let ... lassen
390 everyday ... alltäglich/gewöhnlich

LESSON 74

392 anywhere ... irgendwo / überall
392 somewhere ... irgendwo
392 not anywhere ... nirgendwo
392 nowhere ... nirgendwo
393 loose ... frei / locker / lose
393 loosen ... lockern
393 storm ... Gewitter
393 lightning ... Blitz
393 thunder ... Donner
393 blind ... blind
393 devil ... Teufel
394 ride ... reiten / fahren
394 cycle ... Fahrrad fahren
394 may ... dürfen
394 can ... können
394 could ... könnte
394 permission ... Erlaubnis
394 catch ... fangen / erwischen / einfangen
394 raincoat ... Regenmantel
395 cap ... Hut
395 habit ... Angewohnheit
395 be in the habit of doing . die Angewohnheit haben
396 stranger ... Fremder
396 foreigner ... Ausländer
396 snowstorm ... Schneesturm

LESSON 75

397 look like ... aussehen wie / nach
397 travel ... reisen
397 journey ... Reise
397 just ... einfach/nur
398 of course ... natürlich
398 nowadays ... heutzutage
398 suffer ... leiden
398 wish ... Wunsch
398 exist ... existieren
399 remind ... erinnern
399 in other words ... mit anderen Worten
399 member ... Mitglied
399 library ... Bibliothek
399 even though ... obwohl
399 even ... sogar
399 not even ... nicht einmal
400 to ... zu / in
400 at ... an / in
400 direction ... Richtung
400 soon ... bald
400 at once ... gleich

LESSON 76

402 need ... brauchen
402 towards ... in Richtung / auf etw. zu
402 destination ... Ziel
403 tray ... Tablett
403 stadium ... Stadion
403 much better ... viel besser
403 much more ... viel mehr
403 contrary ... Gegenteil
403 fall ... abfallen / zurückgehen
403 temperature ... Temperatur
403 atmosphere ... Atmosphäre
404 tooth ... Zahn
404 teeth ... Zähne
404 toothbrush ... Zahnbürste
404 dentist ... Zahnarzt
404 seem ... erscheinen/scheinen
404 several ... mehrere
405 compose ... komponieren / verfassen / ... zusammensetzen aus
405 be composed of ... zusammengesetzt aus
405 wise ... klug
405 wisdom ... Weisheit
405 suddenly ... plötzlich
405 pain ... Schmerz
406 certain ... sicher / gewiss
406 pass by ... vorbei laufen
406 park ... Park
406 car park ... Parkplatz
406 picture ... sich vorstellen

LESSON 77

409 diary ... Terminkalender
410 character ... Charakter / Eigenschaft
410 really ... wirklich
410 ran ... lief
410 improve ... verbessern
410 coach ... Trainer/Reisebus
411 flew ... flog
411 wool ... Wolle
412 apostrophe ... Apostroph
412 case ... Fall
412 kick ... treten
413 coast ... Küste
413 certain ... manche
413 tire ... müde werden

Italian Vocabulary

LESSON 61

315 chat........chattare
315 online........online
315 notice........notare
315 free........libero/a, gratis
315 busy........occupato/a, impegnato/a
316 lie........sdraiarsi, giacere
316 comfortable........comodo
316 uncomfortable........scomodo
316 pillow........guanciale
316 wake up – woke up – woken up........svegliarsi
316 go to sleep........andare a dormire
316 immediately........immediatamente
316 midnight........mezzanotte
317 through........attraverso
317 button........bottone
317 buttonhole........asola
317 career........carriera, professione
317 cross........croce
317 crossroads........incroci
317 test........test, prova
318 danger........pericolo
318 dangerous........pericoloso
318 dangerously........pericolosamente
318 alcohol........alcol
318 detective........investigatore
318 should........dovrei
318 obligation........obbligo
318 alternative........alternativa
318 ambulance........ambulanza
319 correct........corretto
319 grammatical........grammaticale
319 problem........problema
319 cause........causa, causare, provocare
319 colleague........collega
319 boss........capo, principale
319 freedom........libertà
319 justice........giustizia
320 as........cosí, siccome, come, poiché
320 that is........cioè
320 bone........osso

LESSON 62

322 life........vita
322 lives........vite
322 the poor........i poveri
322 the rich........i ricchi
322 although........benché, quantunque
322 cook........cucinare
322 tasty........saporito, gustoso
322 pasta........pasta
323 independent........indipendente
323 origin........origine
323 belong to........appartenere a
323 could........potei, potrei
323 vice versa........viceversa
324 throw........lanciare, gettare
324 alive........vivo/a
324 dead........morto/a
324 drop........goccia, cadere, lasciare cadere
324 go without........stare senza
325 assassinate........assassinare
325 usual........solito, consueto
325 unusual........insolito
325 still........ancora
325 yet........non ancora, finora
325 in progress........in corso
326 special........speciale

LESSON 63

327 clean........pulito
327 dirty........sporco
327 dirt........sporcizia
327 know of........essere a conoscenza di...
327 to be afraid........avere paura, temere
328 guard........proteggersi
328 on your guard........stare attenti, stare in guardia
328 off your guard........non stare attenti,
........non stare in guardia
328 calm........calmare, calmo/a
328 quietly........tranquillamente, piano
328 if I were........se fossi ...
328 king........re
328 person (1st, 2nd person etc.)........persona
........(prima pers., seconda pers., ecc.)
329 if I were you, ...se fossi in te
329 advice........consiglio
329 expression........espressione
329 especially........specialmente
330 win – won – won........vincere, vinsi, vinto
330 lottery........lotteria
330 useful........utile
330 useless........inutile
330 possess........possedere
331 take by surprise........prendere di sorpresa

LESSON 64

332 contract........contrarsi
333 sandwich........sandwich
333 cheese........formaggio
333 fault........difetto, errore
333 faultless........senza errori
333 faulty........difettoso
333 fix........correggere
334 OK........va bene, OK
334 all right........va bene
334 compare........paragonare
334 comparison........paragone, confronto
334 have something in common........avere
........qualcosa in comune
334 ice........ghiaccio
334 cool........fresco
334 pour........versare
335 unite........unire
335 even........anche, nemmeno, persino
335 surprising........sorprendente
335 mix........mescolare
335 mixture........miscuglio
335 pink........rosa
335 care........cura
335 care for........avere cura di
335 take care of........prendersi cura di
336 appointment........appuntamento
336 keep an appointment........rispettare

.... un appuntamento
336 hurry .... affrettarsi, avere fretta
336 take your time .... prenditi il tuo tempo
336 plenty of .... abbondanza di

LESSON 65

338 for .... per
338 since .... da, da quando
338 period .... periodo
338 point .... punto
339 kitchen .... cucina
339 fridge .... frigorifero
339 freezer .... congelatore
339 cooker .... fornelli
339 sink .... acquaio
339 microwave .... microonde
339 studies .... studi
340 lend – lent – lent .... prestare, prestai, prestato
340 return .... restituire
340 first name .... nome
340 surname .... cognome
340 actor .... attore
340 actress .... attrice
340 famous .... famoso
340 film star .... divo del cinema
341 industrial .... industriale
341 agricultural .... agricolo
341 region .... regione
341 apologize .... scusarsi
341 apology .... scusa
341 keep somebody waiting .... fare aspettare
.... qualcuno
341 avoid .... evitare
341 bend .... abbassarsi, piegarsi
342 century .... secolo
342 fashion .... moda
342 gate .... cancello
342 worry .... preoccuparsi
342 be worried .... essere preoccupato
342 run .... correre

LESSON 66

344 I was speaking .... stavo parlando
344 particular .... particolare
344 while .... mentre
345 earn .... guadagnare
345 formal .... formale
345 informal .... informale
345 jeans .... jeans
345 trainer .... scarpa da ginnastica
345 how do you do? .... piacere (di conoscerla)
346 persuade .... persuadere, convincere
346 hairdresser .... parrucchiere
346 so = very .... così = molto
346 interesting .... interessante
346 exciting .... eccitante
346 grammatically .... grammaticalmente
346 bathroom .... stanza da bagno
346 bath .... vasca da bagno
346 shower .... doccia
346 toilet .... toeletta
346 basin .... bacinella
347 mirror .... specchio
347 reflect .... riflettere
347 active .... attivo
347 passive .... passivo
347 subject .... soggetto
347 object .... oggetto
348 by .... da, di

LESSON 67

350 force .... forzare
350 make somebody do .... forzare qualcuno
.... a fare qualcosa
350 snack .... spuntino
350 break .... pausa
350 biscuit .... biscotto
350 crisps .... patatine
350 to be born .... nascere
351 murder .... omicidio
351 prison .... prigione
351 pupil .... alunno
351 root .... radice
351 memory .... memoria
352 cross .... attraversare
353 think of .... pensare a
353 safe .... sicuro
353 safety .... sicurezza
353 on your own .... da solo/a
353 lay .... giacqui
354 sir .... signore
354 madam .... signora
354 gentleman .... signore
354 lady .... signora
354 customer .... cliente
354 officer .... ufficiale, poliziotto
354 title .... titolo
355 standard .... livello
355 height .... altezza
355 colourful .... colorito, pittoresco

LESSON 68

356 would you say? .... diresti ...? che ne pensi ...?
356 opinion .... opinione
357 get in .... entrare
357 get out of .... uscire da
357 get on .... salire
357 get off .... scendere
357 taxi .... taxi
357 fare .... prezzo di una corsa, biglietto
357 royal .... reale
357 mud .... fango
357 countryside .... campagna
357 crowd .... folla
357 crowded .... affollato
358 captain .... capitano
358 team .... squadra
358 wide .... largo
358 narrow .... stretto
358 flag .... bandiera
358 national .... nazionale
358 grass .... erba
358 live on .... nutrirsi di
359 tower .... torre
359 wet .... bagnarsi, bagnare, bagnato
359 dry .... asciugare, asciutto
359 threw .... gettò, lanciò
359 loud .... alto
359 turn up .... alzare il volume
359 turn down .... abbassare il volume
360 myself .... me stesso (mi)
360 yourself .... te stesso (ti)
360 himself .... se stesso (si)
360 herself .... se stessa (si)
360 itself .... se stesso(a) (si)
360 oneself .... se stesso (si)
360 ourselves .... noi stessi (ci)
360 yourselves .... voi stessi (vi)

360 themselves ....loro stessi (si)
360 consequently ....di conseguenza
360 protect ....proteggere

LESSON 69

362 thorough .... completo
362 thoroughly.................................. completamente
362 accident..incidente
362 by accident .... per sbaglio
363 careful..attento
363 careless .... sbadato
363 carefully .... attentamente
363 carelessly .... negligentemente
363 own... possedere
363 carry on .... continuare
363 retire .... andare in pensione
364 prize...premio
364 too .... anche, pure
364 at least... almeno
364 widely .... ampiamente
364 manner .... maniera, modo
364 pig.. maiale
365 asleep .... addormentato
365 awake .... sveglio
365 hospital .... ospedale
365 nurse .... infermiere
365 purpose .... scopo
365 in order to ... . allo scopo di ...
365 so that................................ in modo che, affinché
365 take exercise .... fare esercizio fisico
366 notice.. avviso
366 lain .... sdraiato
367 point at.. additare
367 point out... mostrare
367 indicate .... indicare
367 grave .... tomba
368 neck... collo
368 flame... fiamma
368 flight .... volo
368 soup.. minestra, zuppa
368 except.. eccetto

LESSON 70

369 may................................. potrei, può darsi, forse
369 might............................... potrei, può darsi, forse
369 palace .... palazzo
369 parliament.. parlamento
370 arrive at .... arrivare a (un punto)
370 point.. punto
370 arrive in................................ arrivare a (un'area)
370 area .... area
370 airport .... aeroporto
370 passport... passaporto
370 café .... caffè
370 owe .... dovere
370 souvenir... souvenir
371 pride .... orgoglio
371 proud .... orgoglioso
371 normal .... normale
371 normally .... normalmente
371 take pride in..................... essere orgoglioso di ...
371 servant... domestico
372 wheel .... ruota
372 lorry .... camion
372 arrow .... freccia
372 centimetre... centimetro
372 metre .... metro
372 beard .... barba
372 true .... vero
372 false .... falso
372 paper (newspaper) .... quotidiano
372 maintain... mantenere
373 it takes .... ci vuole
373 Ireland .... Irlanda
373 amount .... somma
373 amount to .... ammontare a
373 further .... ulteriore, inoltre, extra
373 Sweden .... Svezia
373 in addition .... in aggiunta
373 extra .... extra, aggiuntivo

LESSON 71

375 I had eaten .... avevo mangiato
376 party .... festa, partito politico
376 political .... politico
377 mad .... pazzo, arrabiato, appassionato di
377 crazy .... folle, pazzo
377 UFO .... ufo
377 copy .... copiare, copia
378 influence .... influenza
378 mouse .... topo
378 mice .... topi
378 throat .... gola
378 opportunity...................................... opportunità
378 develop .... sviluppare
378 industry .... industria
378 agriculture... agricoltura
379 print .... stampare
379 sand... sabbia
379 beach.. spiaggia
379 desert .... deserto
379 bell .... campana
379 knock .... bussare
379 pay a visit .... visitare
379 ring .... suonare
379 shout... gridare
380 stick .... bastone
380 walking stick .... bastone da passeggio
380 exclamation mark .... punto esclamativo

LESSON 72

381 reason .... ragione
381 illness .... malattia
381 tiredness.. stanchezza
381 darkness .... oscurità
381 alone... solo
382 already.. già
382 thrown.. gettato
382 in spite of .... nonostante
382 despite... malgrado
383 anyone... qualcuno
383 someone.. qualcuno
383 no one (no-one).................................... nessuno
384 borrow .... prendere a prestito
384 my own .... mio (proprio)
384 emphasize .... enfatizzare
384 skin .... pelle
385 wire .... filo
385 electricity .... elettricità
385 connection .... connessione
385 wireless .... senza fili
385 Wi-Fi .... wi-fi
385 hyphen..................................... tratto d'unione
385 boil .... bollire
385 fry .... friggere
385 roast .... arrostire
385 brick .... mattone
386 as well .... anche

386 too .... anche
386 also .... anche

LESSON 73

387 I will be speaking .... staro parlando
387 inch .... pollice
387 foot .... piede
387 yard .... iarda
388 chain .... catena
388 rise .... sorgere, levarsi
388 constantly .... costantemente
389 belt .... cintura
389 hourly .... ogni ora
389 daily .... ogni giorno, quotidiano
389 weekly .... ogni settimana, settimanale
389 monthly .... ogni mese, mensile
389 yearly .... ogni anno, annuale
390 allow .... permettere
390 let – let – let .... lasciare
390 everyday .... quotidiano

LESSON 74

392 anywhere .... in qualche luogo, da qualche parte
392 somewhere .... da qualche parte
392 not anywhere .... da nessuna parte
392 nowhere .... in nessun luogo
393 loose .... sciolto, libero, ampio
393 loosen .... sciogliersi, allentare
393 storm .... tempesta, bufera
393 lightning .... fulmine
393 thunder .... tuono
393 blind .... cieco, non vedente
393 devil .... diavolo
394 ride .... cavalcare, andare in autobus, ... in bicicletta, ecc.
394 cycle .... andare in bicicletta
394 may .... potere
394 can .... potere
394 could .... potei, potrei
394 permission .... permesso
394 catch .... prendere, acchiappare
394 raincoat .... impermeabile
395 cap .... berretto
395 habit .... abitudine
395 be in the habit of doing .... avere .... l'abitudine di fare …
396 stranger .... estraneo, sconosciuto
396 foreigner .... straniero
396 snowstorm .... bufera di neve

LESSON 75

397 look like .... somigliare a, sembrare
397 travel .... viaggiare
397 journey .... viaggio
397 just .... soltanto, appena
398 of course .... naturalmente
398 nowadays .... oggigiorno
398 suffer .... soffrire
398 wish .... desiderio
398 exist .... esistere
399 remind .... ricordare (a)
399 in other words .... in altre parole
399 member .... membro, socio
399 library .... biblioteca
399 even though .... anche se
399 even .... pure, anche, persino
399 not even .... neanche, nemmeno
400 to .... a (moto a luogo)
400 at .... a, in (stato in luogo)
400 direction .... direzione
400 soon .... presto, fra poco
400 at once .... immediatamente

LESSON 76

402 need .... aver bisogno
402 towards .... verso
402 destination .... destinazione
403 tray .... vassoio
403 stadium .... stadio
403 much better .... molto meglio
403 much more .... molto di più
403 contrary .... contrario
403 fall .... cadere
403 temperature .... temperatura
403 atmosphere .... atmosfera
404 tooth .... dente
404 teeth .... denti
404 toothbrush .... spazzolino da denti
404 dentist .... dentista, odontoiatra
404 seem .... sembrare
404 several .... parecchi, diversi
405 compose .... comporre
405 be composed of .... essere composto di
405 wise .... saggio
405 wisdom .... saggezza
405 suddenly .... improvvisamente, a un tratto
405 pain .... dolore
406 certain .... certo, sicuro
406 pass by .... passare vicino
406 park .... parco
406 car park .... parcheggio
406 picture .... quadro, disegno, pittura, foto

LESSON 77

409 diary .... giornaliero
410 character .... carattere
410 really .... veramente, realmente, davvero
410 ran .... corse
410 improve .... migliorare
410 coach .... allenatore
411 flew .... volai
411 wool .... lana
412 apostrophe .... apostrofo
412 case .... caso
412 kick .... calciare, prendere a calci
413 coast .... costa
413 certain .... certo
413 tire .... stancare(si)

Japanese Vocabulary

LESSON 61

315 chat....................おしゃべりをする, チャットする
315 online..オンライン
315 notice..気が付く
315 free......（仕事から解放されて）自由な；無料の
315 busy..忙しい
316 lie..横たわる
316 comfortable...快適な
316 uncomfortable.................................心地よくない
316 pillow ....枕
316 wake up - woke up - woken up...............目覚める
316 go to sleep..寝入る
316 immediately ....すぐに
316 midnight..真夜中の12時
317 through ....を通して；...を通り抜けて
317 button ....ボタン
317 buttonhole...ボタン穴
317 career ....キャリア
317 cross..........................十字架；十字形；ばってん
317 crossroads..十字路
317 test...テスト
318 danger ....危険
318 dangerous ....危険な
318 dangerously................................... 危険なほどに
318 alcohol ....アルコール
318 detective ....探偵
318 should.................................. ...するべきである
318 obligation ....責務
318 alternative...代わるもの
318 ambulance...救急車
319 correct ....訂正する
319 grammatical...文法的な
319 problem ....問題
319 cause.......................................原因となる；主義
319 colleague ....同僚
319 boss..上司
319 freedom ....自由
319 justice ....正義
320 as..なので
320 that is..................すなわち；もっと正確に言うと
320 bone ....骨

LESSON 62

322 life...命；人生
322 lives ....lifeの複数形
322 the poor .... 貧乏な人たち
322 the rich... 裕福な人たち
322 although.......................................にもかかわらず
322 cook.. 料理する；料理人
322 tasty...おいしい
322 pasta...パスタ
323 independent..独立した
323 origin..起源
323 belong to................ ...に属する；...の所有である
323 could............... canの過去形；...できるであろう
323 vice versa ....逆もまた同様に
324 throw...投げる
324 alive ....生きている
324 dead ....死んでいる
324 drop .... 落とす；落ちる；一滴の
324 go without ....無しで済ませる
325 assassinate ....暗殺する
325 usual..................................いつもの, ありふれた
325 unusual..................普通でない, 変わった, 珍しい
325 still ....依然として
325 yet..今はまだ
325 in progress...進行中の
326 special ....特別な

LESSON 63

327 clean........汚れていない；清潔な；きれいにする
327 dirty..汚れている
327 dirt ....汚れ
327 know of............ ...がある（いる）のを知っている
327 to be afraid ....がこわい；恐れる
328 guard ....守る
328 on your guard ....用心して
328 off your guard ....油断して
328 calm.................................なだめる；穏やかな
328 quietly ....静かに
328 if I were .... もし私が...であったなら
328 king...王
328 person (1st, 2nd person etc.)人称（一人称、二人称など）, 人
329 if I were you, ...もし私があなたなら
329 advice ....助言
329 expression ....表現
329 especially...特に
330 win - won - won .....勝つ；（くじなどに）当たる
330 lottery...宝くじ
330 useful...役に立つ
330 useless ....役に立たない
330 possess ....所有する
331 take by surprise ....不意を付く

LESSON 64

332 contract..短縮する
333 sandwich .... サンドイッチ
333 cheese...チーズ
333 fault................................短所；落度, 欠陥, 過失
333 faultless ....誤りのない
333 faulty..欠陥のある
333 fix...修理する
334 OK ....オーケー
334 all right..申し分ない
334 compare ....比較する
334 comparison...比較
334 have something in common .... 何か共通点がある
334 ice...氷
334 cool..冷やす
334 pour ....注ぐ
335 unite..一体になる
335 even..でさえ
335 surprising.......................驚かせるような, 意外な
335 mix...混ぜる
335 mixture...混合物
335 pink..ピンク
335 care 世話をする；気遣う；（細心の）注意, きにする
335 care for ....の世話をする
335 take care of................ ...の世話をする；気を配る
336 appointment...予約, 約束
336 keep an appointment...... 予約を守る, 約束を守る
336 hurry .... 急ぐ；大慌て

336 take your time ..... ゆっくり時間をかけてする
336 plenty of ..... 充分な

LESSON 65

338 for ..... …の間
338 since ..... …から
338 period ..... 期間
338 point ..... 点, 時点
339 kitchen ..... キッチン
339 fridge ..... 冷蔵庫
339 freezer ..... 冷凍庫
339 cooker ..... 料理用レンジ
339 sink ..... 流し
339 microwave ..... 電子レンジ
339 studies ..... 勉強
340 lend - lent - lent ..... 貸す
340 return ..... 戻す
340 first name ..... （姓に対する）名
340 surname ..... 苗字
340 actor ..... 男優
340 actress ..... 女優
340 famous ..... 有名な
340 film star ..... 映画スター
341 industrial ..... 産業の
341 agricultural ..... 農業の
341 region ..... 地域
341 apologize ..... 謝る
341 apology ..... 謝罪
341 keep somebody waiting ..... 人を待たせる
341 avoid ..... 避ける
341 bend ..... 曲げる
342 century ..... 世紀
342 fashion ..... ファッション
342 gate ..... ゲート, 門
342 worry ..... 心配する
342 be worried ..... 心配している
342 run ..... 走る

LESSON 66

344 I was speaking （過去の時点で）私は話しをしていた
344 particular ..... 特定の
344 while ..... …している間
345 earn ..... かせぐ
345 formal ..... 正式な
345 informal ..... 形式ばらない
345 jeans ..... ジーパン, ジーンズ
345 trainer ..... 運動靴，スニーカー
345 how do you do? ..... 始めまして
346 persuade ..... 説得する
346 hairdresser ..... 美容師
346 so = very ..... こんなに；非常に
346 interesting ..... 興味深い
346 exciting ..... 興奮させるような
346 grammatically ..... 文法的に
346 bathroom ..... 浴室
346 bath ..... 浴槽
346 shower ..... シャワー；にわか雨
346 toilet ..... トイレ
346 basin ..... 洗面台
347 mirror ..... 鏡
347 reflect ..... 反射する；映す
347 active ..... 能動態
347 passive ..... 受動態
347 subject ..... 主語
347 object ..... 目的語
348 by ..... …によって

LESSON 67

350 force ..... …することを強制する
350 make somebody do ..... 人に…をさせる
350 snack ..... 軽食
350 break ..... 休み時間
350 biscuit ..... ビスケット
350 crisps ..... ポテトチップス
350 to be born ..... 生まれる
351 murder ..... 殺人
351 prison ..... 刑務所
351 pupil ..... 生徒
351 root ..... 根
351 memory ..... 記憶力
352 cross ..... 渡る
353 think of ..... …を想像する；考える
353 safe ..... 安全な
353 safety ..... 安全
353 on your own ..... 一人で
353 lay ..... lieの過去形
354 sir ..... だんな様；士官殿；男の先生；…卿
354 madam ..... 奥様
354 gentleman ..... 男の方；紳士
354 lady ..... ご婦人；淑女；…卿夫人
354 customer ..... 客
354 officer ..... 仕官
354 title ..... 敬称
355 standard ..... 標準；普通の
355 height ..... 身長
355 colourful ..... throwの過去形

LESSON 68

356 would you say ..... …と思うか
356 opinion ..... 意見
357 get in ..... （車に）乗る
357 get out of ..... （車から）降りる
357 get on ..... （バスなどに）乗る
357 get off ..... （バスなどから）降りる
357 taxi ..... タクシー
357 fare ..... 料金
357 royal ..... 王室の
357 mud ..... 泥
357 countryside ..... 田舎
357 crowd ..... 群集
357 crowded ..... 混雑した
358 captain ..... キャプテン, 主将；船長
358 team ..... チーム
358 wide ..... 幅が広い
358 narrow ..... 狭い
358 flag ..... 旗
358 national ..... 国家の
358 grass ..... 草
358 live on ..... …を常食とする
359 tower ..... タワー
359 wet ..... 濡れている
359 dry ..... 乾いている；乾かす
359 threw ..... throwの過去形
359 loud ..... 音が大きい
359 turn up ..... 音を大きくする
359 turn down ..... 音を小さくする
360 myself ..... 私自身
360 yourself ..... あなた自身
360 himself ..... 彼自身
360 herself ..... 彼女自身
360 itself ..... それ自身
360 oneself ..... 自分自身
360 ourselves ..... 我々自身
360 yourselves ..... あなた方自身
360 themselves ..... 彼ら自身

360 consequently ... その結果
360 protect ... 保護する

LESSON 69

362 thorough ... 徹底的な
362 thoroughly ... 徹底的に
362 accident ... 事故
362 by accident ... たまたま
363 careful ... 注意深い
363 careless ... 不注意な
363 carefully ... 注意深く
363 carelessly ... 不注意に
363 own ... 所有する
363 carry on ... し続ける
363 retire ... 定年退職する
364 prize ... 賞
364 too ... もまた
364 at least ... 少なくとも
364 widely ... 広範囲にわたって
364 manner ... 行儀；方法
364 pig ... ブタ
365 asleep ... 眠っている
365 awake ... 目がさめている
365 hospital ... 病院
365 nurse ... 看護師
365 purpose ... 目的
365 in order to ... ...するために
365 so that ... ...するために
365 take exercise ... 運動する
366 notice ... 掲示, お知らせ
366 lain ... lieの過去分詞
367 point at ... 指さす
367 point out ... 指摘する
367 indicate ... 示す
367 grave ... 墓
368 neck ... 首
368 flame ... 炎
368 flight ... フライト
368 soup ... スープ
368 except ... を除いて

LESSON 70

369 may ... かもしれない
369 might ... mayの過去形
369 palace ... 宮殿
369 parliament ... （英国の）国会
370 arrive at ... （駅など）に到着する
370 point ... 地点
370 arrive in ... （町など）に到着する
370 area ... エリア
370 airport ... 空港
370 passport ... パスポート
370 café ... コーヒー店, カフェ
370 owe ... を借りている
370 souvenir ... みやげ
371 pride ... 誇り
371 proud ... 誇りをもっている
371 normal ... 普通の
371 normally ... 普通は
371 take pride in ... を誇りに思っている
371 servant ... 使用人
372 wheel ... 車輪
372 lorry ... 大型トラック
372 arrow ... 矢
372 centimetre ... センチメートル
372 metre ... メートル
372 beard ... あごひげ
372 true ... 真実の
372 false ... 誤った
372 paper (newspaper) ... 新聞
372 maintain ... 維持する
373 it takes ... かかる
373 Ireland ... アイルランド
373 amount ... 総計；量
373 amount to ... （量などが）...に達する
373 further ... さらに遠く；それ以上の
373 Sweden ... スウェーデン
373 in addition ... その上に, ...に加えて
373 extra ... 余計に

LESSON 71

375 I had eaten（過去の時点において）私は食べ終わっていた
376 party ... パーティ；政党；一団
376 political ... 政治の
377 mad ... 頭にきて；熱狂して；気が違った
377 crazy ... 頭がおかしい
377 UFO ... UFO（空飛ぶ円盤など）
377 copy ... 書き写す；（本などの）冊
378 influence ... 影響
378 mouse ... ネズミ
378 mice ... mouseの複数形
378 throat ... 喉
378 opportunity ... 機会
378 develop ... 発展する
378 industry ... 産業
378 agriculture ... 農業
379 print ... 印刷する
379 sand ... 砂
379 beach ... 砂浜
379 desert ... 砂漠
379 bell ... ベル
379 knock ... トントンとたたく
379 pay a visit ... 訪問する
379 ring ... ...を鳴らす
379 shout ... 叫ぶ
380 stick ... 棒切れ
380 walking stick ... 杖
380 exclamation mark ... 感嘆符

LESSON 72

381 reason ... 理由
381 illness ... 病気
381 tiredness ... 疲労
381 darkness ... 暗さ
381 alone ... 一人で
382 already ... もう；すでに
382 thrown ... throwの過去分詞形
382 in spite of ... ...にもかかわらず
382 despite ... ...にもかかわらず
383 anyone ... 誰か（否定・疑問文で）
383 someone ... 誰か（肯定文で）
383 no one (no-one) ... 誰も...ない
384 borrow ... 借りる
384 my own ... 私自身の
384 emphasize ... 強調する
384 skin ... 皮膚
385 wire ... ワイヤー
385 electricity ... 電気
385 connection ... 接続
385 wireless ... ワイヤレス
385 Wi-Fi ... Wi-Fi（ワイ・ファイ）
385 hyphen ... ハイフン
385 boil ... ゆでる
385 fry ... 油で炒める；揚げる
385 roast ... （オーブンなどで）焼く
385 brick ... レンガ
386 as well ... なおその上

386 too ... もまた
386 also ... もまた

LESSON 73

387 I will be speaking （未来のある時点で）私は話しているだろう
387 inch ... インチ
387 foot ... フィート
387 yard ... ヤード
388 chain ... 鎖, (首にかける)チェーン；連続的に
388 rise ... 上がる；昇る；増す
388 constantly ... 絶えず
389 belt ... ベルト
389 hourly ... 1時間ごとの
389 daily ... 毎日の
389 weekly ... 毎週の
389 monthly ... 毎月の
389 yearly ... 毎年の
390 allow ... を許す
390 let – let – let ... させる；させてやる
390 everyday ... 日常の

LESSON 74

392 anywhere ... どこかに；どこでも
392 somewhere ... どこかに
392 not anywhere ... どこにも…ない
392 nowhere ... どこも…ない
393 loose ... 解き放たれた；だぶだぶの；ゆるんだ
393 loosen ... ゆるめる
393 storm ... 嵐
393 lightning ... 稲光
393 thunder ... 雷
393 blind ... 盲目の
393 devil ... 悪魔
394 ride ... 乗る
394 cycle ... 自転車に乗る
394 may ... …してよい
394 can ... できる
394 could ... …してもよい
394 permission ... 許可
394 catch ... 捕る, 捕まえる；…に感染する
394 raincoat ... レインコート
395 cap ... （野球帽のような）帽子
395 habit ... 習慣
395 be in the habit of doing ... …する習慣がある
396 stranger ... 見知らぬ人
396 foreigner ... 外人
396 snowstorm ... ふぶき

LESSON 75

397 look like …に見える；…に似ている；…しそうだ
397 travel ... 旅行する
397 journey ... 旅行
397 just ... ただ…だけ
398 of course ... もちろん
398 nowadays ... 今日では
398 suffer ... 苦しむ
398 wish ... 願望
398 exist ... 存在する
399 remind ... 思い起こさせる
399 in other words ... 言い換えれば
399 member ... メンバー
399 library ... 図書館
399 even though ... …にもかかわらず
399 even ... さえ；よりいっそう
399 not even ... …さえない
400 to ... …に向かって
400 at ... …に
400 direction ... 方向
400 soon ... まもなく；早く
400 at once ... すぐに

LESSON 76

402 need ... 必要がある
402 towards ... の方へ
402 destination ... 目的地
403 tray ... トレー, 盆
403 stadium ... スタジアム
403 much better ... ずっといい
403 much more ... よりいっそう, さらに多く
403 contrary ... 反対の
403 fall ... 落ちる；下がる
403 temperature ... 温度
403 atmosphere ... 大気
404 tooth ... 歯
404 teeth ... toothの複数
404 toothbrush ... 歯ブラシ
404 dentist ... 歯医者
404 seem ... のように思われる
404 several ... いくつかの
405 compose ... 作曲する；…を書く
405 be composed of ... 構成される
405 wise ... 賢い
405 wisdom ... 賢明, 知恵, 知識
405 suddenly ... 突然に
405 pain ... 痛み
406 certain ... 確実な
406 pass by ... 通り過ぎる
406 park ... 駐車する
406 car park ... 駐車場
406 picture ... 心に描く

LESSON 77

409 diary ... 日記
410 character ... 性質
410 really ... 本当に
410 ran ... runの過去形
410 improve ... 上達する
410 coach ... コーチ；長距離バス
411 flew ... flyの過去形
411 wool ... 羊毛, ウール
412 apostrophe ... アポストロフィー
412 case ... 格
412 kick ... 蹴る
413 coast ... 沿岸, 海岸
413 certain ... ある一定の, ある種の
413 tire ... 疲れる；あきる

Polish Vocabulary

LESSON 61

315	chat	czatować
315	online	on-line
315	notice	zauważyć, spostrzec
315	free	wolny, darmowy
315	busy	zajęty
316	lie	leżeć
316	comfortable	wygodny
316	uncomfortable	niewygodny
316	pillow	poduszka
316	wake up – woke up – woken up	budzić się
316	go to sleep	iść spać
316	immediately	natychmiast
316	midnight	północ
317	through	przez
317	button	guzik
317	buttonhole	dziurka od guzika
317	career	kariera
317	cross	krzyż, krzyżyk
317	crossroads	skrzyżowanie
317	test	test
318	danger	niebezpieczeństwo
318	dangerous	niebezpieczny
318	dangerously	niebezpiecznie
318	alcohol	alkohol
318	detective	detektyw
318	should	powinien
318	obligation	zobowiązanie
318	alternative	alternatywa
318	ambulance	karetka
319	correct	poprawiać
319	grammatical	gramatyczny
319	problem	problem
319	cause	powodować, przyczyna
319	colleague	współpracownik
319	boss	szef
319	freedom	wolność
319	justice	sprawiedliwość
320	as	ponieważ
320	that is	to jest, tzn.
320	bone	kość

LESSON 62

322	life	życie
322	lives	życia
322	the poor	biedni
322	the rich	bogaci
322	although	chociaż
322	cook	gotować, kucharz
322	tasty	smaczny
322	pasta	makaron
323	independent	niezależny
323	origin	początek, źródło
323	belong to	należeć do
323	could	II i III forma od czas. „can"
323	vice versa	vice versa
324	throw	rzucać
324	alive	żywy
324	dead	nieżywy
324	drop	upuścić, upadać, kropla
324	go without	obejść się bez
325	assassinate	dokonać zamachu
325	usual	zwykły
325	unusual	niezwykły
325	still	jeszcze, wciąż
325	yet	już, jeszcze
325	in progress	w toku
326	special	specjalny

LESSON 63

327	clean	czysty
327	dirty	brudny
327	dirt	brud
327	know of	wiedzieć o
327	to be afraid	obawiać się, bać się
328	guard	chronić, strzec
328	on your guard	na baczności
328	off your guard	nie na baczności
328	calm	uspokoić, spokojny
328	quietly	cicho
328	if I were	gdybym był …
328	king	król
328	person (1st, 2nd person etc.)	osoba
329	if I were you, …	gdybym był tobą …
329	advice	rada
329	expression	wyrażenie
329	especially	szczególnie
330	win – won – won	wygrać
330	lottery	loteria, lotto
330	useful	pożyteczny
330	useless	bezużyteczny
330	possess	posiadać, mieć
331	take by surprise	zaskoczyć

LESSON 64

332	contract	skracać
333	sandwich	kanapka
333	cheese	ser
333	fault	wada, usterka, wina
333	faultless	bez wad, bez błędów
333	faulty	zepsuty, wadliwy
333	fix	naprawić
334	OK	ok
334	all right	w porządku
334	compare	porównać
334	comparison	porównanie
334	have something in common	mieć cechy wspólne
334	ice	lód
334	cool	ochłodzić
334	pour	lać, nalać
335	unite	jednoczyć (się)
335	even	nawet
335	surprising	zaskakujące
335	mix	mieszać
335	mixture	mieszanka
335	pink	różowy
335	care	opiekować się, troszczyć się, przejmować się
335	care for	troszczyć się
335	take care of	opiekować się
336	appointment	spotkanie
336	keep an appointment	przyjść na spotkanie
336	hurry	spieszyć się

336 take your time..........nie śpieszyć się
336 plenty of..........mnóstwo

LESSON 65

338 for..........przez
338 since..........od ...
338 period..........okres
338 point..........moment
339 kitchen..........kuchnia
339 fridge..........lodówka
339 freezer..........zamrażarka
339 cooker..........kuchenka
339 sink..........zlew
339 microwave..........mikrofalówka
339 studies..........studla
340 lend – lent – lent..........pożyczać (komuś)
340 return..........oddać
340 first name..........imię
340 surname..........nazwisko
340 actor..........aktor
340 actress..........aktorka
340 famous..........słynny, sławny
340 film star..........aktor filmowy
341 industrial..........przemysłowy
341 agricultural..........rolniczy
341 region..........region
341 apologize..........przepraszać
341 apology..........przeprosiny
341 keep somebody waiting..........kazać komuś czekać
341 avoid..........unikać
341 bend..........zgiąć, schylać się
342 century..........stulecie
342 fashion..........moda
342 gate..........brama
342 worry..........martwić się
342 be worried..........być zmartwionym
342 run..........biec

LESSON 66

344 I was speaking..........rozmawiałem
344 particular..........konkretny
344 while..........podczas gdy
345 earn..........zarabiać
345 formal..........formalny
345 informal..........nieformalny
345 jeans..........jeansy
345 trainer..........trampek
345 how do you do?..........Jak się Pan/Pani miewa?
346 persuade..........przekonać
346 hairdresser..........fryzjer
346 so..........tak = bardzo
346 interesting..........interesujący
346 exciting..........ekscytujący
346 grammatically..........gramatycznie
346 bathroom..........łazienka
346 bath..........wanna
346 shower..........prysznic
346 toilet..........toaleta
346 basin..........umywalka
347 mirror..........lustro
347 reflect..........odbijać
347 active..........czynny
347 passive..........bierny
347 subject..........podmiot
347 object..........przedmiot, dopełnienie
347 pupil..........uczeń
348 by..........przez

LESSON 67

350 force..........zmuszać
350 make somebody do..........zmuszać kogoś
..........do, sprawiać
350 snack..........przekąska
350 break..........przerwa
350 biscuit..........ciastko
350 crisps..........chipsy
350 to be born..........urodzić się
351 murder..........morderstwo
351 prison..........więzienie
351 pupil..........uczeń
351 root..........korzeń
351 memory..........pamięć
352 cross..........przejść przez
353 think of..........pomyśleć o
353 safe..........bezpieczny
353 safety..........bezpieczeństwo
353 on your own..........samemu
353 lay..........II forma od czas. „to lie"
354 sir..........pan
354 madam..........pani
354 gentleman..........pan
354 lady..........pani
354 customer..........klient
354 officer..........oficer
354 title..........tytuł
355 standard..........standard, standardowy
355 height..........wzrost
355 colourful..........kolorowy

LESSON 68

356 would you say..........powiedziałbyś?
356 opinion..........opinia, pogląd
357 get in..........wsiadać
357 get out of..........wysiadać
357 get on..........wsiadać
357 get off..........wysiadać
357 taxi..........taksówka
357 fare..........opłata
357 royal..........królewski
357 mud..........błoto
357 countryside..........wieś
357 crowd..........tłum
357 crowded..........tłoczny
358 captain..........kapitan
358 team..........drużyna
358 wide..........szeroki
358 narrow..........wąski
358 flag..........flaga
358 national..........narodowy
358 grass..........trawa
358 live on..........żywić się
359 tower..........wieża
359 wet..........mokry
359 dry..........suchy, suszyć
359 threw..........II forma od czas. „to throw"
359 loud..........głośny
359 turn up..........podgłośnić
359 turn down..........ściszyć
360 myself..........ja siebie
360 yourself..........ty siebie
360 himself..........on siebie
360 herself..........ona siebie
360 itself..........ono się
360 oneself..........siebie
360 ourselves..........my siebie
360 yourselves..........wy siebie

360 themselves ... oni siebie
360 consequently ... więc
360 protect ... chronić

LESSON 69

362 thorough ... gruntowny, całkowity
362 thoroughly ... zupełnie, gruntownie
362 accident ... wypadek
362 by accident ... przez przypadek
363 careful ... ostrożny
363 careless ... nieostrożny
363 carefully ... ostrożnie, starannie
363 carelessly ... nieostrożnie, niechlujnie
363 own ... posiadać, być właścicielem
363 carry on ... kontynuować
363 retire ... przejść na emeryturę
364 prize ... nagroda
364 too ... także, też
364 at least ... przynajmniej
364 widely ... szeroko
364 manner ... maniera, sposób
364 pig ... świnia
365 asleep ... śpiący, we śnie
365 awake ... obudzony, na jawie
365 hospital ... szpital
365 nurse ... pielęgniarka
365 purpose ... cel, powód
365 in order to ... w celu aby
365 so that ... w celu aby
365 take exercise ... gimnastykować się
366 notice ... ogłoszenie, komunikat
366 lain ... III forma czasownika "to lie"
367 point at ... wskazać na
367 point out ... wskazać
367 indicate ... wskazać
367 grave ... grób
368 neck ... szyja
368 flame ... płomień
368 flight ... lot
368 soup ... zupa
368 except ... oprócz

LESSON 70

369 may ... może
369 might ... mógłby -aby, -oby, itd
369 palace ... pałac
369 parliament ... parlament
370 arrive at ... przybyć do
370 point ... miejsce
370 arrive in ... przybyć do
370 area ... obszar
370 airport ... lotnisko
370 passport ... paszport
370 café ... kawiarnia
370 owe ... być dłużnym
370 souvenir ... pamiątka
371 pride ... duma
371 proud ... dumny
371 normal ... normalny
371 normally ... normalnie
371 take pride in ... być dumnym z
371 servant ... służący
372 wheel ... koło
372 lorry ... ciężarówka
372 arrow ... strzała
372 centimetre ... centymetr
372 metre ... metr
372 beard ... broda, zarost
372 true ... prawdziwy
372 false ... fałszywy
372 paper (newspaper) ... gazeta
372 maintain ... utrzymywać
373 It takes ... to trwa, to zajmuje, to wymaga
373 Ireland ... Irlandia
373 amount ... kwota, ilość
373 amount to ... wynosić, równać się
373 further ... dalszy, dodatkowy
373 Sweden ... Szwecja
373 in addition ... w dodatku
373 extra ... dodatkowy

LESSON 71

375 I had eaten ... zjadłem, forma zaprzeszła
376 party ... przyjęcie, impreza, partia, grupa
376 political ... polityczny
377 mad ... wściekły, szalony, szaleć za czymś/kimś
377 crazy ... szalony
377 UFO ... ufo
377 copy ... ściągać, kopiować, kopia
378 influence ... wpływ
378 mouse ... mysz
378 mice ... myszy
378 throat ... gardło
378 opportunity ... okazja, sposobność, możliwość
378 develop ... rozwijać
378 industry ... przemysł
378 agriculture ... rolnictwo
379 print ... drukować
379 sand ... piasek
379 beach ... plaża
379 desert ... pustynia
379 bell ... dzwonek
379 knock ... pukać
379 pay a visit ... złożyć wizytę
379 ring ... dzwonić
379 shout ... krzyczeć
380 stick ... kij, patyk
380 walking stick ... laska
380 exclamation mark ... wykrzyknik

LESSON 72

381 reason ... powód
381 illness ... choroba
381 tiredness ... zmęczenie
381 darkness ... ciemność
381 alone ... sam
382 already ... już
382 thrown ... III forma czasownika "to throw"
382 in spite of ... pomimo
382 despite ... pomimo
383 anyone ... ktoś, ktokolwiek
383 someone ... ktoś
383 no one (no-one) ... nikt
384 borrow ... pożyczyć od kogoś
384 my own ... mój własny
384 emphasize ... podkreślać
384 skin ... skóra
385 wire ... drut, kabel, przewód
385 electricity ... elektryczność, prąd
385 connection ... połączenie
385 wireless ... bezprzewodowy
385 Wi-Fi ... Wi-Fi
385 hyphen ... dywiz
385 boil ... gotować
385 fry ... smażyć
385 roast ... piec
385 brick ... cegła
386 as well ... także, też

386 too .... także, też
386 also .... także, też

LESSON 73

387 I will be speaking .... będę mowić
387 inch .... cal
387 foot .... stopa
387 yard .... jard
388 chain .... łańcuch
388 rise .... wznosić się, wschodzić, wzrastać
388 constantly .... ciągle
389 belt .... pasek
389 hourly .... co godzinę, cogodzinny
389 daily .... dziennie
389 weekly .... tygodniowo
389 monthly .... miesięcznie
389 yearly .... rocznie
390 allow .... pozwolić
390 let – let – let .... pozwolić
390 everyday .... codzienny

LESSON 74

392 anywhere .... gdziekolwiek
392 somewhere .... gdzieś
392 not anywhere .... nigdzie
392 nowhere .... nigdzie
393 loose .... luźno, luźny
393 loosen .... rozluźniać
393 storm .... sztorm
393 lightning .... błyskawica
393 thunder .... grzmot
393 blind .... niewidomy
393 devil .... diabeł
394 ride .... jeździć
394 cycle .... jeździć na rowerze
394 may .... mogę
394 can .... mogę
394 could .... mógłbym
394 permission .... pozwolenie
394 catch .... łapać
394 raincoat .... płaszcz przeciwdeszczowy
395 cap .... czapka z daszkiem
395 habit .... zwyczaj
395 be in the habit of doing .... mieć w zwyczaju
396 stranger .... obcy, nieznajomy
396 foreigner .... cudzoziemiec
396 snowstorm .... śnieżyca

LESSON 75

397 look like .... wyglądać jak
397 travel .... podróżować
397 journey .... podróż
397 just .... tylko
398 of course .... oczywiście
398 nowadays .... obecnie
398 suffer .... cierpieć
398 wish .... marzenie, życzenie
398 exist .... istnieć
399 remind .... przypomnieć
399 in other words .... innymi słowy
399 member .... członek
399 library .... biblioteka
399 even though .... chociaż
399 even .... nawet
399 not even .... nawet (nie)
400 to .... do
400 at .... w
400 direction .... kierunek
400 soon .... wkrótce
400 at once .... natychmiast

LESSON 76

402 need .... potrzebować, potrzeba
402 towards .... w kierunku
402 destination .... cel
403 tray .... taca
403 stadium .... stadion
403 much better .... znacznie lepiej
403 much more .... znacznie więcej
403 contrary .... przeciwieństwo
403 fall .... spaść
403 temperature .... temperatura
403 atmosphere .... atmosfera
404 tooth .... ząb
404 teeth .... zęby
404 toothbrush .... szczoteczka do zębów
404 dentist .... dentysta
404 seem .... wydawać się
404 several .... kilka
405 compose .... komponować, ułożyć
405 be composed of .... składać się z
405 wise .... mądry
405 wisdom .... mądrość
405 suddenly .... nagle
405 pain .... ból
406 certain .... pewny
406 pass by .... przechodzić obok
406 park .... parkować
406 car park .... parking
406 picture .... wyobrażać sobie

LESSON 77

409 diary .... pamiętnik, kalendarz
410 character .... charakter
410 really .... naprawdę
410 ran .... II forma od czas. „to run"
410 improve .... polepszyć
410 coach .... trener, autobus
411 flew .... II forma od czas. "to fly"
411 wool .... wełna
412 apostrophe .... apostrof
412 case .... przypadek
412 kick .... kopnąć
413 coast .... wybrzeże
413 certain .... pewny
413 tire .... zmęczyć się

Portuguese Vocabulary

LESSON 61

315 chat......bater-papo
315 online......ligado na internet
315 notice......notar (reparar) / aviso / anúncio
315 free......livre
315 busy......ocupado
316 lie......deitar-se / deitar
316 comfortable......confortável
316 uncomfortable......desconfortável
316 pillow......travesseiro
316 wake up – woke up – woken up......acordar
...... – acordou – acordado
316 go to sleep......ir durmir
316 immediately......imediatamente
316 midnight......meia-noite
317 through......através
317 button......botão
317 buttonhole......buraco de botão
317 career......carreira
317 cross......cruz
317 crossroads......cruzamento
317 test......teste
318 danger......perigo
318 dangerous......perigoso
318 dangerously......perigosamente
318 alcohol......álcool
318 detective......detetive
318 should......deveria
318 obligation......obrigação
318 alternative......alternativa
318 ambulance......ambulância
319 correct......correto
319 grammatical......gramático
319 problem......problema
319 cause......causar / causa (s)
319 colleague......colega
319 boss......chefe
319 freedom......liberdade
319 justice......justiça
320 as......como
320 that is......isto é / ou seja / quer dizer
320 bone......osso

LESSON 62

322 life......vida
322 lives......vidas
322 the poor......os pobres
322 the rich......os ricos
322 although......embora / apesar de
322 cook......cozinhar
322 tasty......saboroso
322 pasta......macarrão
323 independent......independente
323 origin......origem
323 belong to......pertence à
323 could......poderia
323 vice versa......vice-versa
324 throw......jogar (atirar)
324 alive......vivo
324 dead......morto
324 drop......cair, deixar cair / gota
324 go without......ficar sem
325 assassinate......assassinar
325 usual......usual / comum
325 unusual......incomum
325 still......ainda
325 yet......ainda
325 in progress......em progresso
326 special......especial

LESSON 63

327 clean......limpo
327 dirty......sujo
327 dirt......sujeira
327 know of.....saber de / saber sobre (a respeito de)
327 to be afraid......estar com medo
328 guard......prevenir, resguardar, proteger
328 on your guard......ter cuidado (cautela) /
......prevenir-se
328 off your guard......desprevenido
328 calm......acalmar / calmo
328 quietly......calmamente / silenciosamente
328 if I were......Se eu fosse
328 king......rei
328 person (1st, 2nd person etc.)......pessoa
......(primeira, segunda pessoa, etc.)
329 if I were you, ...se eu fosse você
329 advice......conselho
329 expression......expressão
329 especially......especialmente
330 win – won – won......ganha – ganhou – ganho
330 lottery......loteria
330 useful......útil
330 useless......inútil
330 possess......possuir
331 take by surprise......pegar de supresa

LESSON 64

332 contract......contrato
333 sandwich......sanduíche
333 cheese......queijo
333 fault......defeito / falha / culpa
333 faultless......sem defeito / sem culpa
333 faulty......defeituoso
333 fix......consertar
334 OK......ok
334 all right......tudo certo
334 compare......comparar
334 comparison......comparação
334 have something in common......ter algo
......em comum
334 ice......gelo
334 cool......frio / fresco
334 pour......derramar (despejar)
335 unite......unir
335 even......ainda / até
335 surprising......surpreendente
335 mix......misturar
335 mixture......mistura
335 pink......rosa
335 care......tomar conta (importar-se)
335 care for......cuidar
335 take care of......cuidar
336 appointment......encontro (compromisso)

336 keep an appointment.... manter um compromisso
336 hurry .... apressar-se
336 take your time .... vá com calma
336 plenty of............................ muito(a) de / muito (a)
.... / mais que suficiente

LESSON 65

338 for ....por
338 since .... desde
338 period ....período
338 point..ponto
339 kitchen ....cozinha
339 fridge .... geladeira
339 freezer ....freezer
339 cooker...fogão
339 sink .... pia
339 microwave .... microondas
339 studies .... estudos
340 lend – lent – lent..................................emprestar
340 return .... devolver
340 first name...................................... primeiro nome
340 surname ....sobrenome
340 actor ....ator
340 actress .... atriz
340 famous.. famoso
340 film star...................................estrela de cinema
341 industrial ....industrial
341 agricultural... agrícola
341 region .... região
341 apologize .... desculpar-se
341 apology ....desculpa
341 keep somebody waiting................ deixar alguém
.... esperando
341 avoid... evitar
341 bend .... curvar-se
342 century...século
342 fashion .... moda
342 gate .... portão
342 worry...preocupar-se
342 be worried................................estar preocupado
342 run .... correr

LESSON 66

344 I was speaking.........................eu estava falando
344 particular... particular
344 while .... enquanto
345 earn ....ganhar (dinheiro)
345 formal ....formal
345 informal... informal
345 jeans .... jeans
345 trainer .... tênis
345 how do you do?.................................Como vai?
346 persuade .... persuadir
346 hairdresser .... cabeleireiro
346 so.. tão
346 interesting.. interessante
346 exciting .... excitante
346 grammatically .... gramaticalmente
346 bathroom .... banheiro
346 bath .... banho
346 shower.................................. banho de chuveiro
346 toilet.. banheiro
346 basin.. pia do banheiro
347 mirror .... espelho
347 reflect.. refletir
347 active .... ativo
347 passive .... passivo
347 subject .... sujeito
347 object .... objeto
347 pupil... aluno
348 by.. por / pelo / atravéz

LESSON 67

350 force .... força
350 make somebody do ....forçar alguém a .....
350 snack .... lanche / merenda
350 break .... intervalo
350 biscuit .... biscoito
350 crisps .... batatas fritas
350 to be born .... ter nascido
351 murder ....assassinar
351 prison.. prisão
351 pupil... aluno
351 root .... raiz
351 memory .... memória
352 cross .... atravessar
353 think of............ pensar em / pensar a respeito de
353 safe.. seguro
353 safety .... segurança
353 on your own.. sozinho (a)
353 lay... deitou
354 sir... senhor
354 madam .... senhora
354 gentleman... cavalheiro
354 lady.. dama
354 customer... cliente
354 officer.................................. oficial / comandante
354 title... título
355 standard .... padrão
355 height.. altura
355 colourful... colorido

LESSON 68

356 would you say...você diria
356 opinion.. opinião
357 get in.. entrar
357 get out of .... sair
357 get on ....subir / entrar
357 get off .... descer / sair
357 taxi.. táxi
357 fare .... passagem / tarifa
357 royal.. real
357 mud .... lama
357 countryside ....interior
357 crowd .... multidão
357 crowded .... lotado
358 captain.. capitão
358 team ....time
358 wide .... largo
358 narrow .... estreito
358 flag.. bandeira
358 national.. nacional
358 grass... grama
358 live on .... sobrevive / vive
359 tower... torre
359 wet... molhado
359 dry .... seco
359 threw...jogou (atirou)
359 loud..................................... barulhento / alto
359 turn up .... aumentar
359 turn down... abaixar
360 myself .... eu mesmo
360 yourself..você mesmo
360 himself .... ele mesmo
360 herself.. ela mesma
360 itself .... ele mesmo
360 oneself .... alguem
360 ourselves ....nós mesmos

Portuguese vocabulary

360	yourselves	vocês mesmos
360	themselves	eles mesmos
360	consequently	conseqüentemente
360	protect	proteger

LESSON 69

362	thorough	completo (minucioso)
362	thoroughly	completamente (minuciosamente)
362	accident	acidente
362	by accident	por acaso
363	careful	cuidadoso
363	careless	descuidado
363	carefully	cuidadosamente
363	carelessly	descuidadamente
363	own	possuir
363	carry on	continuar
363	retire	aposentar
364	prize	prêmio
364	too	também
364	at least	pelo menos
364	widely	amplamente
364	manner	maneiras (modos)
364	pig	porco
365	asleep	adormecido / durmindo
365	awake	acordado
365	hospital	hospital
365	nurse	enfermeiro
365	purpose	propósito / motivo
365	in order to ...	para
365	so that	para que
365	take exercise	fazer exercício
366	notice	aviso / anúncio
366	lain	deitado
367	point at	apontar
367	point out	indicar (distinguir)
367	indicate	indicar
367	grave	túmulo
368	neck	pescoço
368	flame	chama
368	flight	vôo
368	soup	sopa
368	except	exceto

LESSON 70

369	may	poder (possibilidade)
369	might	poder (possibilidade – para segundo condicional)
369	palace	palácio
369	parliament	parlamento
370	arrive at	chegar ao
370	point	ponto
370	arrive in	chegar no
370	area	area
370	airport	aeroporto
370	passport	passaporte
370	café	cafeteria
370	owe	dever
370	souvenir	souvenir
371	pride	orgulho
371	proud	orgulhoso
371	normal	normal
371	normally	normalmente
371	take pride in	ter orgulho em
371	servant	empregado / serviçal
372	wheel	roda
372	lorry	caminhão
372	arrow	flecha
372	centimetre	centímetro
372	metre	metro
372	beard	barba
372	true	verdade
372	false	falso
372	paper (newspaper)	jornal
372	maintain	manter
373	it takes	leva, demora
373	Ireland	Irlanda
373	amount	quantia
373	amount to	resultar em, totalizar
373	further	além de (mais longe)
373	Sweden	Suécia
373	in addition	além disso
373	extra	extra

LESSON 71

375	I had eaten	Eu havia comido
376	party	festa / grupo / partido
376	political	político
377	mad	bravo / muito interessado em / louco
377	crazy	louco
377	UFO	ovni (ufo)
377	copy	copiar
378	influence	influência
378	mouse	rato
378	mice	ratos
378	throat	garganta
378	opportunity	oportunidade
378	develop	desenvolver
378	industry	indústria
378	agriculture	agricultura
379	print	imprimir
379	sand	areia
379	beach	praia
379	desert	deserto
379	bell	sino
379	knock	bater
379	pay a visit	visitar
379	ring	tocar
379	shout	gritar
380	stick	bastão / taco
380	walking stick	bengala
380	exclamation mark	ponto de exclamação

LESSON 72

381	reason	razão
381	illness	doença
381	tiredness	cansaço
381	darkness	escuridão
381	alone	sozinho (a)
382	already	já
382	thrown	atirado
382	in spite of	apesar de
382	despite	apesar de
383	anyone	alguém
383	someone	alguém
383	no one (no-one)	ninguém
384	borrow	pegar emprestado
384	my own	pertence à mim
384	emphasize	enfatizar
384	skin	pele
385	wire	cabo
385	electricity	eletricidade
385	connection	conexão
385	wireless	sem fio
385	Wi-Fi	Wi-Fi
385	hyphen	hífen
385	boil	ferver
385	fry	fritar
385	roast	assar

385 brick.............tijolo
386 as well.............também
386 too.............também
386 also.............também

LESSON 73

387 I will be speaking.............Estarei falando
387 inch.............polegada
387 foot.............pé
387 yard.............jarda
388 chain.............corrente
388 rise.............levantar / subir / nascer (do sol)
388 constantly.............constantemente
389 belt.............cinto
389 hourly.............por hora
389 daily.............diariamente
389 weekly.............semanalmente
389 monthly.............mensalmente
389 yearly.............anualmente
390 allow.............permitir
390 let – let – let.............permitir – permitiu – permitido
390 everyday.............todos os dias

LESSON 74

392 anywhere.............qualquer lugar
392 somewhere.............algum lugar
392 not anywhere.............nenhum lugar
392 nowhere.............lugar nenhum
393 loose.............solto / frouxo
393 loosen.............soltar / afrouxar
393 storm.............tempestade
393 lightning.............raio / relâmpago
393 thunder.............trovão
393 blind.............cego
393 devil.............diabo
394 ride.............cavalgar / andar de (ônibus, bicicleta)
394 cycle.............andar de bicicleta
394 may.............poder
394 can.............poder
394 could.............pôde
394 permission.............permissão
394 catch.............apanhar (pegar)
394 raincoat.............capa de chuva
395 cap.............boné
395 habit.............hábito
395 be in the habit of doing.............estar acostumado à
396 stranger.............estranho
396 foreigner.............estrangeiro
396 snowstorm.............tempestade de neve

LESSON 75

397 look like.............paracer, parecerse
397 travel.............viajar
397 journey.............viagem
397 just.............apenas
398 of course.... é claro / naturalmente / seguramente
398 nowadays.............atualmente, hoje em dia
398 suffer.............sofrer
398 wish.............desejar
398 exist.............existir
399 remind.............fazer lembrar
399 in other words.............em outras palavras
399 member.............membro
399 library.............biblioteca
399 even though.............embora
399 even.............ainda / mesmo / e até
399 not even.............mesmo que / mesmo por
400 to.............para
400 at.............em / no
400 direction.............direção
400 soon.............logo
400 at once.............imediatamente

LESSON 76

402 need.............precisar
402 towards.............em direção à
402 destination.............destino
403 tray.............bandeja
403 stadium.............estádio
403 much better.............muito melhor
403 much more.............muito mais
403 contrary.............contrário
403 fall.............cair
403 temperature.............temperatura
403 atmosphere.............atmosfera
404 tooth.............dente
404 teeth.............dentes
404 toothbrush.............escova de dentes
404 dentist.............dentista
404 seem.............parecer
404 several.............vários (muitos)
405 compose.............compor
405 be composed of.............ser composto de
405 wise.............sábio (adjetivo)
405 wisdom.............sabedoria
405 suddenly.............repentinamente
405 pain.............dor
406 certain.............certo (certeza)
406 pass by.............passar por
406 park.............estacionar / parque
406 car park.............estacionamento
406 picture.............imaginar

LESSON 77

409 diary.............diário, agenda
410 character.............caráter
410 really.............realmente
410 ran.............correu
410 improve.............melhorar
410 coach.............treinador
411 flew.............voou
411 wool.............lã
412 apostrophe.............apóstrofo
412 case.............caso
412 kick.............chutar
413 coast.............costa
413 certain.............particular / específico
413 tire.............cansar

Russian Vocabulary

LESSON 61

315 chat .... разговаривать, болтать
315 online .... онлайн
315 notice .... замечать
315 free .... свободный, бесплатный
315 busy .... занятый
316 lie .... лежать
316 comfortable .... удобный
316 uncomfortable .... неудобный
316 pillow .... подушка
316 wake up - woke up - woken up .... просыпаться - проснулся - проснулся
316 go to sleep .... ложиться спать
316 immediately .... немедленно
316 midnight .... полночь
317 through .... сквозь
317 button .... пуговица
317 buttonhole .... петля
317 career .... карьера
317 cross .... крестик
317 crossroads .... перекресток
317 test .... контрольная работа
318 danger .... опасность
318 dangerous .... опасный
318 dangerously .... опасно
318 alcohol .... алкоголь
318 detective .... детектив
318 should .... следует
318 obligation .... обязательство
318 alternative .... альтернатива , выбор
318 ambulance .... скорая помощь
319 correct .... исправлять
319 grammatical .... грамматический
319 problem .... проблема
319 cause .... вызывать,быть причиной; причина, ... мотив цель (for the causes of = ради)
319 colleague .... коллега
319 boss .... начальник
319 freedom .... свобода
319 justice .... справедливость
320 as .... так как
320 that is .... то есть
320 bone .... кость

LESSON 62

322 life .... жизнь
322 lives .... жизни
322 the poor .... бедные
322 the rich .... богатые
322 although .... хотя
322 cook .... готовить, повар
322 tasty .... вкусный
322 pasta .... паста
323 independent .... независимый
323 origin .... происхождение
323 belong to .... принадлежать
323 could .... мог бы
323 vice versa .... наоборот
324 throw .... бросать
324 alive .... живой
324 dead .... мертвый
324 drop .... ронять, капля
324 go without .... обходиться без
325 assassinate .... убивать
325 usual .... обычный
325 unusual .... необычный
325 still .... все еще
325 yet .... еще не
325 in progress .... в процессе
326 special .... особенный

LESSON 63

327 clean .... чистый
327 dirty .... грязный
327 dirt .... грязь
327 know of .... знать о
327 to be afraid .... бояться
328 guard .... защищаться, охранять
328 on your guard .... быть бдительным
328 off your guard .... потерять бдительность
328 calm .... спокойный, успокаивать
328 quietly .... тихо
328 if I were .... если бы я был ...
328 king .... король
328 person (1st, 2nd person etc.) .... лицо (1-е, 2-е лицо и т.д.)
329 if I were you, ... на твоем/ .... вашем месте, я бы
329 advice .... совет
329 expression .... выражение
329 especially .... особенно
330 win - won - won .... победить - победил - победил, ... выиграть - выиграл - выиграл
330 lottery .... лотерея
330 useful .... полезный
330 useless .... бесполезный
330 possess .... обладать
331 take by surprise .... застигнуть врасплох

LESSON 64

332 contract .... сокращать
333 sandwich .... бутерброд
333 cheese .... сыр
333 fault .... ошибка, недостаток, вина
333 faultless .... безупречный, невиновный, ... безошибочный
333 faulty .... неисправный
333 fix .... починить
334 OK .... ОК, хорошо
334 all right .... все в порядке
334 compare .... сравнивать
334 comparison .... сравнение
334 have something in common .... иметь что-то общее
334 ice .... лед
334 cool .... охлаждать
334 pour .... наливать
335 unite .... объединяться
335 even .... даже
335 surprising .... удивительный
335 mix .... смешивать
335 mixture .... смесь
335 pink .... розовый

335 care ... заботиться
335 care for ... заботиться о
335 take care of ... заботиться о
336 appointment ... назначенная встреча
336 keep an appointment ... приходить на назначенную встречу
336 hurry ... спешить, спешка
336 take your time ... не спешите
336 plenty of ... много

LESSON 65

338 for ... в течение
338 since ... начиная с
338 period ... период
338 point ... момент
339 kitchen ... кухня
339 fridge ... холодильник
339 freezer ... морозилка
339 cooker ... плита для приготовления пищи
339 sink ... раковина (мойка)
339 microwave ... микроволновая печь
339 studies ... учеба, занятия
340 lend - lent - lent ... одалживать - одалживал - одолжил
340 return ... возвращать
340 first name ... имя
340 surname ... фамилия
340 actor ... актер
340 actress ... актриса
340 famous ... знаменитый
340 film star ... кинозвезда
341 industrial ... промышленный
341 agricultural ... сельскохозяйственный
341 region ... регион, область
341 apologize ... извиняться
341 apology ... извинение
341 keep somebody waiting ... заставлять кого-то ждать
341 avoid ... избегать
341 bend ... сгибать
342 century ... столетие
342 fashion ... мода
342 gate ... ворота
342 worry ... беспокоиться
342 be worried ... быть обеспокоенным
342 run ... бежать

LESSON 66

344 I was speaking ... я говорил
344 particular ... конкретный
344 while ... пока
345 earn ... зарабатывать (деньги)
345 formal ... формальный, официальный
345 informal ... неформальный
345 jeans ... джинсы
345 trainer ... кроссовок
345 how do you do? ... здравствуйте
346 persuade ... убеждать
346 hairdresser ... парикмахер
346 so = very ... очень
346 interesting ... интересный
346 exciting ... волнующий
346 grammatically ... грамматически
346 bathroom ... ванная (комната)
346 bath ... ванна
346 shower ... душ
346 toilet ... туалет
346 basin ... раковина (для умывания)
347 mirror ... зеркало
347 reflect ... отражать
347 active ... активный
347 passive ... пассивный
347 subject ... подлежащее
347 object ... дополнение
348 by ... предлог ... (присоединяет субъект действия)

LESSON 67

350 force ... принуждать
350 make somebody do ... заставлять кого-либо делать ...
350 snack ... легкая закуска
350 break ... перерыв
350 biscuit ... бисквит, печенье
350 crisps ... чипсы
350 to be born ... родиться
351 murder ... убийство
351 prison ... тюрьма
351 pupil ... ученик
351 root ... корень
351 memory ... память
352 cross ... пересекать
353 think of ... думать о
353 safe ... безопасный
353 safety ... безопасность
353 on your own ... самостоятельно
353 lay ... лежал
354 sir ... сэр
354 madam ... мадам
354 gentleman ... джентльмен
354 lady ... леди
354 customer ... клиент
354 officer ... офицер
354 title ... обращение, титул
355 standard ... стандарт, стандартный
355 height ... рост
355 colourful ... цветной

LESSON 68

356 would you say ... как вы думаете?
356 opinion ... мнение
357 get in ... садиться в
357 get out of ... выходить из
357 get on ... садиться на
357 get off ... выходить из
357 taxi ... такси
357 fare ... плата за проезд
357 royal ... королевский
357 mud ... грязь
357 countryside ... сельская местность
357 crowd ... толпа
357 crowded ... переполненный людьми
358 captain ... капитан
358 team ... команда
358 wide ... широкий
358 narrow ... узкий
358 flag ... флаг
358 national ... национальный
358 grass ... трава
358 live on ... жить на
359 tower ... башня
359 wet ... мокрый
359 dry ... сухой, сушиться
359 threw ... бросил
359 loud ... громкий
359 turn up ... включать звук
359 turn down ... уменьшать звук
360 myself ... себя

360 yourself .... себя (ты)
360 himself .... себя (он)
360 herself .... себя (она)
360 itself .... себя (оно)
360 oneself .... себя
360 ourselves .... себя (мы)
360 yourselves .... себя (вы)
360 themselves .... себя (они)
360 consequently .... следовательно
360 protect .... защищать

LESSON 69

362 thorough .... тщательный
362 thoroughly .... совершенно
362 accident .... несчастный случай
362 by accident .... случайно
363 careful .... осторожный
363 careless .... беззаботный
363 carefully .... внимательно
363 carelessly .... беззаботно
363 own .... владеть
363 carry on .... продолжать
363 retire .... уходить на пенсию
364 prize .... приз
364 too .... тоже
364 at least .... по меньшей мере
364 widely .... широко
364 manner .... способ, манера
364 pig .... свинья
365 asleep .... спящий
365 awake .... бодрствующий
365 hospital .... больница
365 nurse .... медсестра
365 purpose .... цель
365 in order to ... . для того чтобы ...
365 so that .... чтобы
365 take exercise .... упражняться
366 notice .... объявление
366 lain .... лег
367 point at .... указывать на
367 point out .... обращать внимание, указывать
367 indicate .... указывать
367 grave .... могила
368 neck .... шея
368 flame .... пламя
368 flight .... полет, рейс
368 soup .... суп
368 except .... за исключением

LESSON 70

369 may .... может
369 might .... мог (бы)
369 palace .... дворец
369 parliament .... парламент
370 arrive at .... прибывать на/в/к
370 point .... точка, место
370 arrive in .... прибывать в
370 area .... местность, зона
370 airport .... аэропорт
370 passport .... паспорт
370 café .... кафе
370 owe .... быть должным
370 souvenir .... сувенир
371 pride .... гордость
371 proud .... гордый
371 normal .... нормальный
371 normally .... обычно
371 take pride in .... гордиться чем-либо
371 servant .... слуга
372 wheel .... колесо
372 lorry .... грузовик
372 arrow .... стрела
372 centimetre .... сантиметр
372 metre .... метр
372 beard .... борода
372 true .... правдивый
372 false .... фальшивый, ложный
372 paper (newspaper) .... газета
372 maintain .... обслуживать, содержать
373 it takes .... требуется
373 Ireland .... Ирландия
373 amount .... количество
373 amount to .... равняться, составлять в сумме
373 further .... дальше; дополнительный
373 Sweden .... Швеция
373 in addition .... в дополнение
373 extra .... дополнительный

LESSON 71

375 I had eaten .... я съел
376 party .... вечеринка, партия, группа людей
376 political .... политический
377 mad .... сумасшедший
377 crazy .... сумасшедший
377 UFO .... НЛО
377 copy .... копировать, списывать, копия
378 influence .... влияние
378 mouse .... мышь
378 mice .... мыши
378 throat .... горло
378 opportunity .... возможность
378 develop .... развивать
378 industry .... промышленность
378 agriculture .... сельское хозяйство
379 print .... печатать
379 sand .... песок
379 beach .... пляж
379 desert .... пустыня
379 bell .... звонок, колокол
379 knock .... стучать
379 pay a visit .... наносить визит
379 ring .... звонить
379 shout .... кричать
380 stick .... палка
380 walking stick .... трость
380 exclamation mark .... восклицательный знак

LESSON 72

381 reason .... причина
381 illness .... болезнь
381 tiredness .... усталость
381 darkness .... темнота
381 alone .... один
382 already .... уже
382 thrown .... бросил
382 in spite of .... несмотря на
382 despite .... несмотря на
383 anyone .... кто-либо
383 someone .... кто-то
383 no one (no-one) .... никто
384 borrow .... брать в долг
384 my own .... мой собственный
384 emphasize .... усиливать, подчеркивать
384 skin .... кожа
385 wire .... провод
385 electricity .... электричество
385 connection .... связь
385 wireless .... беспроводной

385 Wi-Fi ... Wi-Fi, беспроводной доступ в интернет
385 hyphen ... дефис
385 boil ... варить
385 fry ... жарить
385 roast ... жарить, запекать
385 brick ... кирпич
386 as well ... также
386 too ... также
386 also ... также

LESSON 73

387 I will be speaking ... я буду говорить
387 inch ... дюйм
387 foot ... фут
387 yard ... ярд
388 chain ... цепь
388 rise ... подниматься, возрастать
388 constantly ... постоянно
389 belt ... пояс, ремень
389 hourly ... ежечасный, ежечасно
389 daily ... ежедневный, ежедневно
389 weekly ... еженедельный, еженедельно
389 monthly ... ежемесячный, ежемесячно
389 yearly ... ежегодный, ежегодно
390 allow ... позволять
390 let – let – let ... позволять — позволил — позволил
390 everyday ... повседневный

LESSON 74

392 anywhere ... м
392 somewhere ... где-то
392 not anywhere ... нигде
392 nowhere ... нигде
393 loose ... свободный, незакрепленный
393 loosen ... ослаблять, отпускать
393 storm ... буря, гроза
393 lightning ... молния
393 thunder ... гром
393 blind ... слепой
393 devil ... дьявол
394 ride ... ездить на чем-либо
394 cycle ... ездить на велосипеде
394 may ... мочь, иметь разрешение делать что-лбо
394 can ... мочь,уметь, быть способным
394 could ... мог, мог бы
394 permission ... разрешение
394 catch ... поймать, ловить
394 raincoat ... плащ
395 cap ... кепка
395 habit ... привычка
395 be in the habit of doing ... иметь привычку делать что-либо
396 stranger ... незнакомец
396 foreigner ... иностранец
396 snowstorm ... снежная буря

LESSON 75

397 look like ... выглядеть как, быть похожим
397 travel ... путешествовать
397 journey ... путешествие
397 just ... только
398 of course ... конечно
398 nowadays ... в наше время
398 suffer ... страдать
398 wish ... желание
398 exist ... существовать
399 remind ... напоминать
399 in other words ... иначе говоря
399 member ... член
399 library ... библиотека
399 even though ... даже если
399 even ... даже
399 not even ... даже не
400 to ... к, в (предлог направления)
400 at ... в, возле
400 direction ... направление
400 soon ... скоро
400 at once ... сразу же

LESSON 76

402 need ... нуждаться
402 towards ... по направлению к
402 destination ... место назначения
403 tray ... поднос
403 stadium ... стадион
403 much better ... намного лучше
403 much more ... намного больше
403 contrary ... противоположность
403 fall ... падать
403 temperature ... температура
403 atmosphere ... атмосфера
404 tooth ... зуб
404 teeth ... зубы
404 toothbrush ... зубная щетка
404 dentist ... стоматолог
404 seem ... казаться
404 several ... несколько
405 compose ... сочинять, составлять
405 be composed of ... состоять из
405 wise ... мудрый
405 wisdom ... мудрость
405 suddenly ... неожиданно
405 pain ... боль
406 certain ... уверенный
406 pass by ... проходить мимо
406 park ... парковать
406 car park ... автомобильная стоянка, парковка
406 picture ... изображать

LESSON 77

409 diary ... ежедневник
410 character ... характер
410 really ... действительно
410 ran ... бежал
410 improve ... улучшать
410 coach ... тренер, автобус (междугородного сообщения)
411 flew ... летел
411 wool ... шерсть
412 apostrophe ... апостроф
412 case ... падеж
412 kick ... пинать, ударять ногой
413 coast ... побережье
413 certain ... определенный
413 tire ... уставать

Slovak Vocabulary

LESSON 61

315 chat ... rozprávať sa
315 online ... online, prostredníctvom internetu
315 notice ... všimnúť si
315 free ... voľný, zadarmo
315 busy ... zaneprázdnený
316 lie ... ležať
316 comfortable ... pohodlný
316 uncomfortable ... nepohodlný
316 pillow ... vankúš
316 wake up - woke up - woken up ... zobudiť sa
... (základný tvar) – zobudiť sa (minulý čas)
... – zobudiť sa (príčastie minulé)
316 go to sleep ... ísť spať
316 immediately ... okamžite, ihneď
316 midnight ... polnoc
317 through ... cez
317 button ... gombík
317 buttonhole ... gombíková dierka
317 career ... kariéra
317 cross ... kríž, krížik
317 crossroads ... križovatka
317 test ... test
318 danger ... nebezpečenstvo
318 dangerous ... nebezpečný
318 dangerously ... nebezpečne
318 alcohol ... alkohol
318 detective ... detektív
318 should ... mal by
318 obligation ... povinnosť
318 alternative ... alternatíva, voľba
318 ambulance ... sanitka
319 correct ... opraviť, opravovať
319 grammatical ... gramatický
319 problem ... problém
319 cause ... príčina, zapríčiniť
319 colleague ... kolega
319 boss ... šéf
319 freedom ... sloboda
319 justice ... spravodlivosť
320 as ... keďže
320 that is ... to je, to jest
320 bone ... kosť

LESSON 62

322 life ... život
322 lives ... životy
322 the poor ... chudobní ľudia
322 the rich ... bohatí ľudia, boháči
322 although ... hoci
322 cook ... variť, kuchár
322 tasty ... chutný
322 pasta ... cestoviny
323 independent ... nezávislý
323 origin ... pôvod
323 belong to ... patriť niekomu
323 could ... mohol by ...
323 vice versa ... naopak, obrátene
324 throw ... hodiť, hádzať
324 alive ... živý, nažive
324 dead ... mŕtvy
324 drop ... pustiť, padať, kvapka
324 go without ... zaobísť sa bez
325 assassinate ... zavraždiť
325 usual ... zvyčajný, bežný
325 unusual ... nezvyčajný
325 still ... stále, ešte
325 yet ... ešte (v otázke a zápore)
325 in progress ... v procese
326 special ... zvláštny, mimoriadny

LESSON 63

327 clean ... čistý, čistiť
327 dirty ... špinavý
327 dirt ... špina
327 know of ... poznať niečo, vedieť o niečom
327 to be afraid ... báť sa
328 guard ... chrániť sa
328 on your guard ... na pozore
328 off your guard ... nedávať si pozor
328 calm ... upokojiť, pokojný
328 quietly ... potichu
328 if I were ... Keby som bol ...
328 king ... kráľ
328 person (1st, 2nd person etc.) ... osoba
... (1., 2. osoba, atď.)
329 if I were you, ... Keby som bol
... na tvojom mieste ...
329 advice ... rada
329 expression ... výraz
329 especially ... najmä, predovšetkým
330 win - won - won ... vyhrať
... (základný tvar) – vyhrať (minulý čas)
... – vyhrať (príčastie minulé)
330 lottery ... lotéria
330 useful ... užitočný
330 useless ... zbytočný
330 possess ... mať, vlastniť
331 take by surprise ... prekvapiť /nečakane/

LESSON 64

332 contract ... skrátiť
333 sandwich ... sendvič
333 cheese ... syr
333 fault ... chyba
333 faultless ... bez chyby, bezchybný
333 faulty ... chybný, poruchový
333 fix ... napraviť
334 OK ... OK, dobre
334 all right ... v poriadku
334 compare ... porovnať
334 comparison ... porovnanie
334 have something in common ... mať niečo
... spoločné
334 ice ... ľad
334 cool ... vychladiť
334 pour ... liať
335 unite ... spojiť sa, zjednotiť
335 even ... dokonca
335 surprising ... prekvapujúci
335 mix ... miešať, zmiešať
335 mixture ... zmes
335 pink ... ružová
335 care ... starostlivosť

335 care for .... záležať na, starať sa o
335 take care of .... postarať sa o
336 appointment .... stretnutie
336 keep an appointment .... dodržať čas stretnutia
336 hurry .... ponáhľať sa
336 take your time ...... neponáhľať sa, dávať si načas
336 plenty of .... veľa, mnoho

LESSON 65

338 for .... po dobu, počas
338 since .... od určitej doby
338 period .... doba, obdobie
338 point .... bod
339 kitchen .... kuchyňa
339 fridge .... chladnička
339 freezer .... mraznička
339 cooker .... sporák
339 sink .... umývadlo, výlevka
339 microwave .... mikrovlnná rúra
339 studies .... štúdium
340 lend - lent - lent požičať (základný tvar) – požičať .... (minulý čas) – požičať (príčastie minulé)
340 return .... vrátiť
340 first name .... meno
340 surname .... priezvisko
340 actor .... herec
340 actress .... herečka
340 famous .... slávny
340 film star .... filmová hviezda
341 industrial .... priemyselný
341 agricultural .... poľnohospodársky
341 region .... región
341 apologize .... ospravedlniť sa
341 apology .... ospravedlnenie
341 keep somebody waiting ..... nechať niekoho čakať
341 avoid .... vyhnúť sa
341 bend .... skloniť, zohnúť sa
342 century .... storočie
342 fashion .... móda
342 gate .... brána
342 worry .... obávať sa
342 be worried .... mať obavy
342 run .... bežať

LESSON 66

344 I was speaking .... Hovoril som
344 particular .... určitý
344 while .... zatiaľ čo, kým
345 earn .... zarobiť
345 formal .... formálny
345 informal .... neformálny
345 jeans .... džínsy
345 trainer .... teniska
345 how do you do? .... teší ma
346 persuade .... presvedčiť
346 hairdresser .... kaderník, kaderníčka
346 so = very .... tak = veľmi
346 interesting .... zaujímavý
346 exciting .... vzrušujúci
346 grammatically .... gramaticky
346 bathroom .... kúpeľňa
346 bath .... vaňa
346 shower .... sprcha
346 toilet .... záchod
346 basin .... umývadlo
347 mirror .... zrkadlo
347 reflect .... odrážať
347 active .... aktívny
347 passive .... trpný
347 subject .... podmet (gramatický)
347 object .... predmet (gramatický)
348 by .... do určitého času

LESSON 67

350 force .... nútiť
350 make somebody do .... prinútiť/zapríčiniť, že .... niekto niečo urobí
350 snack .... rýchle občerstvenie
350 break .... prestávka, pauza
350 biscuit .... keks
350 crisps .... zemiakové lupienky
350 to be born .... narodiť sa
351 murder .... vražda
351 prison .... väzenie
351 pupil .... žiak
351 root .... koreň
351 memory .... pamäť
352 cross .... prejsť cez
353 think of .... pomyslieť si
353 safe .... bezpečný
353 safety .... bezpečnosť
353 on your own .... (ty) sám
353 lay .... minulý čas slovesa ležať (lie)
354 sir .... pán, pane
354 madam .... pani
354 gentleman .... pán
354 lady .... pani, Lady
354 customer .... zákazník
354 officer .... dôstojník
354 title .... titul
355 standard .... úroveň
355 height .... výška
355 colourful .... pestrofarebný

LESSON 68

356 would you say .... povedal by si
356 opinion .... názor
357 get in .... nastúpiť (do auta)
357 get out of .... vystúpiť (z auta)
357 get on .... nastúpiť .... (do autobusu, vlaku, lietadla, na loď)
357 get off .... vystúpiť .... (z autobusu, vlaku, lietadla, lode)
357 taxi .... taxík
357 fare .... cestovné
357 royal .... kráľovský
357 mud .... blato
357 countryside .... príroda, vidiek
357 crowd .... dav
357 crowded .... preplnený
358 captain .... kapitán
358 team .... tím
358 wide .... široký
358 narrow .... úzky
358 flag .... vlajka
358 national .... národný
358 grass .... tráva
358 live on .... živiť sa /niečím/
359 tower .... veža
359 wet .... mokrý
359 dry .... suchý
359 threw .... minulý čas slovesa hodiť (throw)
359 loud .... nahlas
359 turn up .... zosilniť
359 turn down .... stlmiť
360 myself .... (ja) seba, sebe
360 yourself .... (ty) seba, sebe
360 himself .... (on) seba, sebe

360 herself........(ona) seba, sebe
360 itself........(ono, to) seba, sebe
360 oneself........seba, sebe
360 ourselves........(my) seba, sebe
360 yourselves........(vy) seba, sebe
360 themselves........(oni) seba, sebe
360 consequently........preto
360 protect........ochrániť

LESSON 69

362 thorough........dôkladný
362 thoroughly........dôkladne, úplne
362 accident........nehoda
362 by accident........náhodou, omylom
363 careful........opatrný
363 careless........neopatrný
363 carefully........opatrne
363 carelessly........neopatrne
363 own........vlastniť
363 carry on........pokračovať
363 retire........ísť do dôchodku
364 prize........cena (výhra)
364 too........tiež
364 at least........najmenej
364 widely........široko, veľmi
364 manner........spôsob, mrav
364 pig........prasa
365 asleep........spiaci
365 awake........zobudený
365 hospital........nemocnica
365 nurse........zdravotná sestra
365 purpose........účel
365 in order to ....aby ...
365 so that........aby
365 take exercise........cvičiť
366 notice........oznámenie
366 lain........minulé príčastie slovesa ležať (lie)
367 point at........ukázať na niečo (prstom)
367 point out........poukázať na niečo
367 indicate........označiť
367 grave........hrob
368 neck........krk
368 flame........plameň
368 flight........let
368 soup........polievka
368 except........okrem

LESSON 70

369 may........smieť, môcť
369 might........smieť, môcť
369 palace........palác
369 parliament........parlament
370 arrive at........prísť na nejaké miesto
370 point........miesto
370 arrive in........prísť do nejakej oblasti
370 area........oblasť
370 airport........letisko
370 passport........pas
370 café........kaviareň
370 owe........dlžiť
370 souvenir........suvenír
371 pride........pýcha
371 proud........pyšný, hrdý
371 normal........normálny, bežný
371 normally........normálne, bežne
371 take pride in........byť hrdý na niečo,
........pýšiť sa niečim
371 servant........sluha
372 wheel........koleso
372 lorry........nákladné auto
372 arrow........šíp
372 centimetre........centimeter
372 metre........meter
372 beard........brada /z fúzov/
372 true........pravdivý
372 false........nepravdivý
372 paper (newspaper)........noviny
372 maintain........udržovať
373 it takes........trvá to
373 Ireland........Írsko
373 amount........suma, množstvo
373 amount to........rovnať sa, dosahovať hodnotu
373 further........ďalej, extra
373 Sweden........Švédsko
373 in addition........navyše
373 extra........extra

LESSON 71

375 I had eaten ..... Jedol som (predtým, ako sa niečo stalo)
376 party........oslava, strana (politická)
376 political........politický
377 mad........zúrivý, zbláznený, šialený
377 crazy........bláznivý
377 UFO........UFO
377 copy........opisovať, kopírovať, kópia
378 influence........vplyv
378 mouse........myš
378 mice........myši
378 throat........hrdlo
378 opportunity........príležitosť, možnosť
378 develop........rozvíjať
378 industry........priemysel
378 agriculture........poľnohospodárstvo
379 print........tlačiť
379 sand........piesok
379 beach........pláž
379 desert........púšť
379 bell........zvonček
379 knock........klopať, zaklopať
379 pay a visit........navštíviť
379 ring........zvoniť, zazvoniť
379 shout........kričať
380 stick........palica
380 walking stick........vychádzková palica
380 exclamation mark........výkričník

LESSON 72

381 reason........dôvod
381 illness........choroba
381 tiredness........únava
381 darkness........tma
381 alone........sám
382 already........už
382 thrown....... minulé príčastie slovesa hodiť (throw)
382 in spite of........napriek niečomu
382 despite........napriek niečomu
383 anyone........niekto (v otázke), nikto (v zápore)
383 someone........niekto (v kladnej vete)
383 no one (no-one)........nikto (v kladnej vete)
384 borrow........požičať si
384 my own........môj vlastný
384 emphasize........zdôrazniť
384 skin........koža
385 wire........drôt
385 electricity........elektrina
385 connection........spojenie
385 wireless........bezdrôtový

Slovak vocabulary

385 Wi-Fi ... Wi-Fi
385 hyphen ... pomlčka
385 boil ... uvariť
385 fry ... smažiť
385 roast ... piecť
385 brick ... tehla
386 as well ... tiež
386 too ... tiež
386 also ... tiež

LESSON 73

387 I will be speaking ... Budem hovoriť
387 inch ... palec (britská dĺžková jednotka)
387 foot ... stopa (britská dĺžková jednotka)
387 yard ... yard (dĺžková miera)
388 chain ... retiazka, reťaz
388 rise ... vychádzať, stúpať
388 constantly ... neustále
389 belt ... opasok
389 hourly ... hodinový, každú hodinu
389 daily ... denný
389 weekly ... týždenný
389 monthly ... mesačný
389 yearly ... ročný
390 allow ... dovoliť, povoliť
390 let – let – let ... dovoliť (základný tvar) – dovoliť ... (minulý čas) – dovoliť (príčastie minulé)
390 everyday ... každý deň

LESSON 74

392 anywhere ... niekde (v otázke)
392 somewhere ... niekde (v kladnej vete)
392 not anywhere ... nikde (v zápore)
392 nowhere ... nikde (v kladnej vete)
393 loose ... nepriviazaný, voľný, uvoľnený
393 loosen ... uvoľniť
393 storm ... búrka
393 lightning ... blýskanie
393 thunder ... hrom
393 blind ... slepý
393 devil ... čert, diabol
394 ride ... jazdiť, voziť sa
394 cycle ... bicyklovať
394 may ... smieť, môcť
394 can ... môcť
394 could ... mohol by ...
394 permission ... povolenie
394 catch ... chytiť
394 raincoat ... pršiplášť
395 cap ... šiltovka
395 habit ... zvyk
395 be in the habit of doing ... zvyknúť niečo robiť
396 stranger ... cudzí človek
396 foreigner ... cudzinec
396 snowstorm ... snehová búrka

LESSON 75

397 look like ... vyzerať ako
397 travel ... cestovať
397 journey ... cesta
397 just ... len, iba
398 of course ... samozrejme
398 nowadays ... v súčasnosti
398 suffer ... trpieť
398 wish ... želanie, prianie
398 exist ... existovať
399 remind ... pripomenúť
399 in other words ... inými slovami
399 member ... člen
399 library ... knižnica
399 even though ... aj keď
399 even ... dokonca
399 not even ... dokonca ani
400 to ... k, do (smerom niekam)
400 at ... v (niekde)
400 direction ... smer
400 soon ... skoro, čoskoro
400 at once ... hneď

LESSON 76

402 need ... potrebovať
402 towards ... smerom k
402 destination ... cieľ
403 tray ... podnos
403 stadium ... štadión
403 much better ... oveľa lepšie
403 much more ... oveľa viac
403 contrary ... opak
403 fall ... klesať
403 temperature ... teplota
403 atmosphere ... atmosféra
404 tooth ... zub
404 teeth ... zuby
404 toothbrush ... zubná kefka
404 dentist ... zubár
404 seem ... zdať sa, vyzerať
404 several ... niekoľko
405 compose ... skladať, vytvoriť
405 be composed of ... byť zložený z
405 wise ... múdry
405 wisdom ... múdrosť, rozum
405 suddenly ... náhle
405 pain ... bolesť
406 certain ... istý
406 pass by ... prejsť okolo
406 park ... parkovať
406 car park ... parkovisko
406 picture ... predstavovať si

LESSON 77

409 diary ... diár
410 character ... charakter, povaha
410 really ... naozaj, skutočne
410 ran ... minulý čas slovesa bežať (run)
410 improve ... zlepšiť, zdokonaliť
410 coach ... tréner, autobus
411 flew ... minulý čas slovesa letieť (fly)
411 wool ... vlna
412 apostrophe ... apostrof
412 case ... spôsob (gramatický)
412 kick ... kopnúť
413 coast ... pobrežie
413 certain ... určitý
413 tire ... unaviť (sa)

Spanish Vocabulary

LESSON 61

315 chat ... charlar, hablar
315 online ... por internet
315 notice ... notar, darse cuenta
315 free ... gratis
315 busy ... ocupado/a/os/as
316 lie ... estar/yacer un objeto en un sitio; echarse, ... acostarse, tenderse, tumbarse (persona)
316 comfortable ... cómodo/a/os/as
316 uncomfortable ... incómodo/a/os/as
316 pillow ... almohada
316 wake up – woke up – woken up ... despertar, ... despertarse
316 go to sleep ... dormirse
316 immediately ... inmediatamente, de inmediato
316 midnight ... medianoche
317 through ... a través de
317 button ... botón
317 buttonhole ... ojal
317 career ... carrera (profesional)
317 cross ... cruz
317 crossroads ... cruce
317 test ... prueba, test
318 danger ... peligro
318 dangerous ... peligroso/a/os/as
318 dangerously ... peligrosamente
318 alcohol ... alcohol
318 detective ... detective
318 should ... debería, deberías, debería, ... deberíamos, deberíais, deberían
318 obligation ... obligación
318 alternative ... alternativa
318 ambulance ... ambulancia
319 correct ... correcto/a/os/as
319 grammatical ... gramatical/es
319 problem ... problema
319 cause ... causar; causa
319 colleague ... compañero/a, colega
319 boss ... jefe, jefa
319 freedom ... libertad
319 justice ... justicia
320 as ... como, ya que, puesto que
320 that is ... es decir
320 bone ... hueso

LESSON 62

322 life ... vida
322 lives ... vidas
322 the poor ... los pobres
322 the rich ... los ricos
322 although ... aunque
322 cook ... cocinar; cocinero/a
322 tasty ... sabroso/a/os/as
322 pasta ... pasta
323 independent ... independiente/s
323 origin ... origen
323 belong to ... pertenecer a
323 could ... pasado del verbo 'can' (poder)
323 vice versa ... viceversa
324 throw ... lanzar, tirar
324 alive ... vivo/a/os/as
324 dead ... muerto/a/os/as
324 drop ... dejar caer, tirar; gota
324 go without ... pasar sin
325 assassinate ... asesinar
325 usual ... habitual/es, usual/es
325 unusual ... poco corriente/es, ... poco común/comunes, inusual/es
325 still ... todavía, aún
325 yet ... todavía, aún
325 in progress ... en proceso, se está desarrollando
326 special ... especial/es

LESSON 63

327 clean ... limpio/a/os/as
327 dirty ... sucio/a/os/as
327 dirt ... suciedad
327 know of ... conocer
327 to be afraid ... tener miedo
328 guard ... prevenir, custodiar; guardia
328 on your guard ... estar alerta/s, ... estar prevenido/a/os/as
328 off your guard ... no estar alerta/s, estar ... desprevenido/a/os/as
328 calm ... calmar (verbo); calma (nombre)
328 quietly ... en silencio, sin hacer ruido; ... tranquilamente
328 if I were ... si (yo) + verbo (segundo ... condicional), por ejemplo ... 'si yo fuera/fuese, tuviera/tuviese,...
328 king ... rey
328 person (1st, 2nd person etc.) ... persona verbal ... (primera, segunda, etc)
329 if I were you, ... si yo fuera/fuese tú,...
329 advice ... consejo
329 expression ... expresión
329 especially ... en especial, especialmente
330 win – won – won ... ganar
330 lottery ... lotería
330 useful ... útil/es
330 useless ... inútil/es
330 possess ... poseer
331 take by surprise ... pillar por sorpresa

LESSON 64

332 contract ... contraer
333 sandwich ... sándwich, bocadillo
333 cheese ... queso
333 fault ... defecto, culpa, falta
333 faultless ... impecable, perfecto, ... sin defectos, sin culpa
333 faulty ... defectuoso/a/os/as
333 fix ... corregir, arreglar
334 OK ... vale, de acuerdo, bien
334 all right ... vale, de acuerdo, bien
334 compare ... comparar
334 comparison ... comparación
334 have something in common ... tener algo ... en común
334 ice ... hielo
334 cool ... enfriar
334 pour ... verter, echar, servir
335 unite ... unir(se)
335 even ... incluso

335 surprising ... sorprendente
335 mix ... mezclar
335 mixture ... mezcla
335 pink ... rosa (color)
335 care ... cuidar
335 care for ... cuidar de
335 take care of ... cuidar de
336 hurry ... apresurarse, darse prisa
336 take your time ... tomarse tiempo
336 appointment ... cita
336 keep an appointment ... mantener una cita
336 plenty of ... mucho, cantidad de

LESSON 65

338 for ... durante
338 since ... desde
338 period ... período, espacio de tiempo
338 point ... punto
339 kitchen ... cocina
339 fridge ... frigorífico, nevera
339 freezer ... congelador
339 sink ... fregadera
339 microwave ... microondas
339 cooker ... cocina (electrodoméstico)
339 studies ... estudios
340 lend – lent – lent ... prestar
340 return ... devolver (objeto), volver (persona)
340 first name ... nombre de pila
340 surname ... apellido
340 actor ... actor
340 actress ... actriz
340 famous ... famoso/a/os/as
340 film star ... estrella de cine
341 industrial ... industrial/es
341 agricultural ... agrícola/s
341 region ... región
341 apologize ... disculparse, pedir disculpas
341 apology ... disculpa
341 keep somebody waiting ... hacer esperar ... a alguien
341 avoid ... evitar
341 bend ... doblar(se)
342 century ... siglo
342 fashion ... moda
342 gate ... puerta
342 worry ... preocupar(se)
342 be worried ... estar preocupado/a/os/as
342 run ... correr

LESSON 66

344 I was speaking ... (yo) estaba hablando
344 particular ... concreto/a/os/as, particular/es
344 while ... mientras
345 earn ... ganar
345 formal ... formal/es
345 informal ... informal/es
345 jeans ... (pantalón) vaquero, ... (pantalones) vaqueros
345 trainer ... zapatillas de deporte
345 how do you do? ... much gusto, encantado
346 persuade ... persuadir
346 hairdresser ... peluquero/a
346 so ... tan
346 interesting ... interesante/s
346 exciting ... emocionante/s, excitante/s
346 grammatically ... gramaticalmente
346 bathroom ... (cuarto de) baño, servicio, aseo
346 bath ... baño
346 shower ... ducha
346 toilet ... (cuarto de) baño, servicio, aseo
346 basin ... lavabo
347 mirror ... espejo
347 reflect ... reflejar(se)
347 active ... (voz) activa
347 passive ... (voz) pasiva
347 subject ... sujeto
347 object ... objeto
347 pupil ... alumno/a
348 by ... por (voz pasiva)

LESSON 67

350 force ... forzar
350 make somebody do ... forzar a alguien a hacer ...
350 snack ... tentempié, algo de picar
350 break ... pausa, descanso
350 biscuit ... galleta
350 crisps ... patatas fritas (de bolsa)
350 to be born ... nacer
351 murder ... asesinato
351 prison ... prisión
351 pupil ... alumno/a
351 root ... raíz
351 memory ... memoria
352 cross ... cruzar
353 think of ... pensar en
353 safe ... seguro/a/os/as
353 safety ... seguridad
353 on your own ... solo/a/os/as
353 lay ... pasado del verbo 'to lie' (tumbarse, ... estar tumbado, acostarse, estar acostado)
354 sir ... señor
354 madam ... señora
354 gentleman ... caballero, señor
354 lady ... señora, dama
354 customer ... cliente
354 officer ... oficial
354 title ... título
355 standard ... estándar
355 height ... altura
343 colourful ... vistoso/a/os/as, ... lleno/a/os/as de color

LESSON 68

356 would you say ... ¿Dirías (tú)?, ... ¿Te parece (a ti)?, ¿Opinas (tú)?
356 opinion ... opinión
357 get in ... subirse a (un coche), entrar en
357 get out of ... bajarse de (un coche), salir de
357 get on ... subirse a (un autobús, ... tren, avión o barco)
357 get off ... bajarse de (un autobús, ... tren, avión o barco)
357 taxi ... taxi
357 fare ... billete (para viajar), pasaje
357 royal ... real/es (de la realeza)
357 mud ... barro
357 countryside ... campo, campiña
357 crowd ... gentío, muchedumbre, ... multitud (de gente), el público
357 crowded ... abarrotado, atestado, ... lleno de gente
358 captain ... capitán/capitana
358 team ... equipo
358 wide ... ancho/a/os/as
358 narrow ... estrecho/a/os/as
358 flag ... bandera
358 national ... nacional/es
358 grass ... hierba, césped

358 live on ... alimentarse principalmente de
359 tower ... torre
359 wet ... mojado/a/os/as, húmedo/a/os/as
359 dry ... seco/a/os/as (adjetivo)
359 threw ... pasado del verbo 'to throw' (tirar, lanzar)
359 loud ... fuerte/s, alto/a/os/as (refiriéndose a sonido)
359 turn up ... subir (la música, el volumen de la tele, radio,...)
359 turn down ... bajar (la música, el volumen de la tele, radio,...)
360 myself ... yo mismo/a, (tras preposición) mí mismo/a
360 yourself ... tú mismo/a, (tras preposición) ti mismo/a
360 himself ... él mismo, (tras preposición) sí mismo
360 herself ... ella misma, (tras preposición) sí misma
360 itself ... reflexivo para cosas, (tras preposición) sí mismo/a (depende del género de la cosa)
360 oneself ... uno/a mismo/a, (tras preposición) sí mismo/a
360 ourselves ... nosotros/as mismos/as, a nosotros/as mismos/as
360 yourselves ... vosotros/as mismos/as, a vosotros/as mismos/as
360 themselves ... ellos/as mismos/as, a ellos/as mismos/as
360 consequently ... por consiguiente, consiguientemente
360 protect ... proteger

LESSON 69

362 thorough ... a fondo, completo/a/os/as
362 thoroughly ... a fondo, completamente
362 accident ... accidente
362 by accident ... por accidente
363 careful ... cuidadoso/a/os/as
363 careless ... descuidado/a/os/as, despreocupado/a/os/as
363 carefully ... con cuidado, cuidadosamente
363 carelessly ... de manera despreocupada, sin la debida atención
363 own ... poseer (verbo)
363 carry on ... seguir (haciendo algo), continuar
363 retire ... jubilarse, retirarse
364 prize ... premio
364 too ... también
364 at least ... al menos, por lo menos
364 widely ... ampliamente, extensamente
364 manner ... modales, manera, modo
364 pig ... cerdo
365 asleep ... dormido/a/os/as
365 awake ... despierto/a/os/as
365 hospital ... hospital
365 nurse ... enfermero/a
365 purpose ... propósito, intención
365 in order to ... para, con el propósito/la intención
365 so that ... para, con el propósito/la intención
365 take exercise ... hacer ejercicio
366 notice ... letrero, aviso
366 lain ... participio pasado del verbo 'to lie' (estar/ yacer un objeto en un sitio; echarse, acostarse, tenderse, tumbarse (persona))
367 point at ... señalar, indicar (con el dedo, físicamente)
367 point out ... señalar, poner de relieve, destacar (algo entre otras cosas)
367 indicate ... indicar
367 grave ... tumba (nombre)
368 neck ... cuello
368 flame ... llama
368 flight ... vuelo, trayectoria
368 soup ... sopa
368 except ... excepto, a parte de

LESSON 70

369 may ... puede que
369 might ... podría
369 palace ... palacio
369 parliament ... parlamento
370 arrive at ... llegar a (un punto concreto, como un edificion o una estación)
370 point ... punto concreto
370 arrive in ... llegar a (un área, como una ciudad o un país)
370 area ... área
370 airport ... aeropuerto
370 passport ... pasaporte
370 café ... cafetería, café (lugar)
370 owe ... deber (dinero, una explicación)
370 souvenir ... recuerdo (objeto)
371 pride ... orgullo
371 proud ... orgulloso/a/os/as
371 normal ... normal/es
371 normally ... normalmente
371 take pride in ... estar orgulloso/a/os/as de, tomarse en serio algo que se hace
371 servant ... sirviente, criado
372 wheel ... rueda
372 lorry ... camión
372 arrow ... flecha
372 centimetre ... centímetro
372 metre ... metro
372 beard ... barba
372 true ... verdadero/a/os/as
372 false ... falso/a/os/as
372 paper (newspaper) ... periódico
372 maintain ... mantener, sostener
373 it takes ... cuesta (en términos de tiempo, esfuerzo)
373 ireland ... Irlanda
373 amount ... cantidad
373 amount to ... sumar, ascender a (cantidad)
373 further ... más, más lejos
373 Sweden ... Suecia
373 in addition ... además
373 extra ... extra

LESSON 71

375 I had eaten ... (yo) había comido
376 party ... fiesta, partido (político), grupo
376 political ... político/a/os/as
377 mad ... enfadado/a/os/as; loco/a/os/as; muy interesado/a/os/as
377 crazy ... enfadado/a/os/as; loco/a/os/as; muy interesado/a/os/as
377 UFO ... ovni
377 copy ... copiar (verbo), copia (nombre)
378 influence ... influencia
378 mouse ... ratón
378 mice ... ratones
378 throat ... garganta
378 opportunity ... oportunidad
378 develop ... desarrollar

378	industry	industria
378	agriculture	agricultura
379	print	imprimir
379	sand	arena
379	desert	desierto
379	beach	playa
379	bell	campana, timbre
379	knock	golpear (con los nudillos), llamar a la puerta
379	pay a visit	hacer una visita, visitar (a alguien)
379	ring	llamar (al timbre de una puerta)
379	shout	gritar, chillar
380	stick	palo
380	walking stick	bastón
368	exclamation mark	signo de admiración

LESSON 72

381	reason	razón, causa
381	illness	enfermedad
381	tiredness	cansancio
381	darkness	oscuridad
381	alone	solo/a/os/as
382	already	ya
382	thrown	participio pasado del verbo 'to throw' (tirar, lanzar)
382	in spite of	a pesar de
382	despite	a pesar de
383	anyone	(= anybody) alguien (en preguntas), nadie (en frases negativas)
383	someone	(= somebody) alguien
383	no one (no-one)	(= nobody) nadie
384	borrow	tomar prestado
384	my own	mi propio/a/os/as (seguido de un nombre)
384	emphasize	poner de relieve
384	skin	piel
385	wire	cable
385	electricity	electricidad
385	connection	conexión
385	wireless	inalámbrico/a/os/as
385	Wi-Fi	wifi', conexión inalámbrica
385	hyphen	guión (ortográfico)
385	boil	hervir
385	fry	freír
385	roast	asar
385	brick	ladrillo
386	as well	también
386	too	también
386	also	también

LESSON 73

387	I will be speaking	(futuro continuo o progresivo en inglés) hablaré
387	inch	pulgada
387	foot	pie
387	yard	yarda
388	chain	cadena
388	rise	elevarse, subir (algo por si mismo)
388	constantly	constantemente
389	belt	cinturón
389	hourly	por/cada hora
389	daily	al/por/cada día, todos los días, diariamente
389	weekly	a la/por/cada semana, todas las semanas, semanalmente
389	monthly	al/por/cada mes, todos los meses, mensualmente
389	yearly	al/por/cada año, todos los años, anualmente
390	allow	permitir, dejar
390	let – let – let	permitir, dejar
390	everyday	todos los días

LESSON 74

392	anywhere	(en preguntas) a/en algún lugar/sitio/lado, a/en alguna parte; en cualquier lugar/sitio/lado/parte
392	somewhere	(en frases afirmativas) a/en algún lugar/sitio/lado, a/en alguna parte; en cualquier lugar/sitio/lado/parte
392	not anywhere	(en frases negativas) a/en ningún lugar/sitio/lado, a/en ninguna parte
392	nowhere	(en frases negativas) a/en ningún lugar/sitio/lado, a/en ninguna parte
393	loose	suelto/a/os/as
393	loosen	soltar, dejar suelto, aflojar
393	storm	tormenta
393	lightning	rayo, relámpago
393	thunder	trueno
393	blind	ciego/a/os/as
393	devil	demonio, diablo
394	ride	montar a (caballo), montar o andar en (bicicleta, moto), viajar en (autobús, metro, tren)
394	cycle	montar o andar en (bicicleta)
394	may	puedo, podría (en una pregunta pidiendo permiso, registro formal)
394	can	puedo (en una pregunta pidiendo permiso, registro normal)
394	could	puedo, podría (en una pregunta pidiendo permiso, registro formal)
394	permission	permiso
394	catch	coger
394	raincoat	gabardina, impermeable
395	cap	gorra
395	habit	hábito, costumbre
395	be in the habit of doing	tener (la) costumbre de hacer
396	stranger	desconocido/a (nombre)
396	foreigner	extranjero/a (nombre)
396	snowstorm	ventisca, tormenta de nieve

LESSON 75

397	look like	parecerse; parecer que (va a suceder algo)
397	travel	viajar
397	journey	viaje
397	just	sólo, solamente
398	of course	por supuesto
398	nowadays	hoy en día
398	suffer	sufrir
398	wish	deseo
398	exist	existir
399	remind	recordar (a alguien algo)
399	in other words	es decir, dicho de otro modo
399	member	miembro
399	library	biblioteca
399	even though	incluso si
399	even	incluso
399	not even	ni siquiera
400	to	a, hacia
400	at	en
400	direction	dirección
400	soon	pronto
400	at once	inmediatamente, de inmediato

LESSON 76

402 need .... necesitar
402 towards.. hacia
402 destination .... destino
403 tray .... bandeja
403 stadium.. estadio
403 much better .... mucho mejor
403 much more .... mucho más
403 contrary .... opuesto, contrario
403 fall.. caer
403 temperature .... temperatura
403 atmosphere .... atmósfera, ambiente
404 tooth .... diente
404 teeth .... dientes
404 toothbrush .... cepillo de dientes
404 dentist... dentista
404 seem... parecer
404 several.. varios/as
405 compose.. componer
405 be composed of........ estar compuesto/a/os/as de
405 wise .... prudente/s, acertado/a/os/as,
.... sensato/a/os/as
405 wisdom .... sabiduría
405 suddenly .... de repente
405 pain.. dolor
406 certain... seguro/a/os/as
406 pass by .... pasar, pasar por
406 park .... aparcar (verbo), parque (nombre)
406 car park .... aparcamiento
406 picture............ imaginarse (verbo), foto (nombre)

LESSON 77

409 diary.. diario (nombre)
410 character .... carácter
410 really.. muy + adjetivo
410 ran .... pasado del verbo 'to run' (correr)
410 improve.. mejorar
410 coach...................... entrenador, autobús, autocar
411 flew .... pasado del verbo 'to fly' (volar)
411 wool .... lana
412 apostrophe .... apóstrofe
412 case.. caso
412 kick .... dar una patada/patadas
413 coast.. costa
413 certain... seguro/a/os/as
413 tire .... cansarse

Turkish Vocabulary

LESSON 61

315 chat ... sohbet etmek
315 online ... çevrim içi
315 notice ... fark etmek
315 free ... serbest/bedava
315 busy ... meşgul
316 lie ... uzanmak
316 comfortable ... rahat
316 uncomfortable ... rahatsız
316 pillow ... yastık
316 wake up - woke up - woken up.. uyanmak (3 hali)
316 go to sleep ... uyumaya gitmek
316 immediately ... anında
316 midnight ... gece yarısı
317 through ... Içinden/...-den
317 button ... düğme
317 buttonhole ... düğme deliği
317 career ... kariyer
317 cross ... çarpı
317 crossroads ... kavşak
317 test ... test
318 danger ... tehlike
318 dangerous ... tehlikeli
318 dangerously ... tehlikeli bir şekilde
318 alcohol ... alkol
318 detective ... detektif
318 should ... -meli/ -malı
318 obligation ... mecburiyet
318 alternative ... alternatif
318 ambulance ... ambülans
319 correct ... düzeltmek
319 grammatical ... dil bilgisine ait
319 problem ... problem
319 cause ... neden olmak/neden
319 colleague ... iş arkadaşı
319 boss ... patron
319 freedom ... özgürlük
319 justice ... adalet
320 as ... Err:509
320 that is ... yani
320 bone ... kemik

LESSON 62

322 life ... hayat
322 lives ... hayatlar
322 the poor ... fakirler
322 the rich ... zenginler
322 although ... 'sına rağmen
322 cook ... yemek pişirmek
322 tasty ... lezzetli
322 pasta ... makarna
323 independent ... bağımsız
323 origin ... köken
323 belong to ... 'e ait olmak
323 could ... -ebilirdi/ 'can' geçmiş zaman hali
323 vice versa ... tersine
324 throw ... fırlatmak
324 alive ... hayatta
324 dead ... ölü
324 drop ... düşürmek/damla
324 go without ... -sız idare etmek
325 assassinate ... suikast yapmak
325 usual ... olağan
325 unusual ... olağan dışı
325 still ... hala
325 yet ... henüz
325 in progress ... devam etmekte
326 special ... özel

LESSON 63

327 clean ... temiz
327 dirty ... kirli
327 dirt ... kir
327 know of ... bilmek
327 to be afraid ... korkmak
328 guard ... korunmak
328 on your guard ... tetikte
328 off your guard ... hazırlıksız yakalanmak
328 calm ... sakinleştirmek/sakin
328 quietly ... sessizce
328 if I were ...Eğer ... olsaydım...2. şartlı cümlelerde kullanılır
328 king ... kral
328 person (1st, 2nd person etc.) ...şahıs (1. şahıs, 2. şahıs, vb.)
329 if I were you, ... Eğer senin yerinde olsaydım...
329 advice ... tavsiye
329 expression ... ifade
329 especially ... özellikle
330 win - won - won ... kazanmak
330 lottery ... piyango
330 useful ... kullanışlı /yararlı
330 useless ... işe yaramaz/faydasız
330 possess ... sahip olmak
331 take by surprise ... gafil avlamak

LESSON 64

332 contract ... kısaltmak
333 sandwich ... sandviç
333 cheese ... peynir
333 fault ... hata
333 faultless ... hatasız
333 faulty ... hatalı şekilde
333 fix ... düzeltmek
334 OK ... TAMAM
334 all right ... tamam
334 compare ... karşılaştırmak
334 comparison ... karşılaştırma
334 have something in commonortak bir şeyleri olmak
334 ice ... buz
334 cool ... soğutmak
334 pour ... dökmek (içecek)
335 unite ... birleşmek
335 even ... bile
335 surprising ... şaşırtıcı
335 mix ... karıştırmak
335 mixture ... karışım
335 pink ... pembe
335 care ... ilgilenmek
335 care for ... -e bakmak/ ilgilenmek
335 take care of ... bakımını üstlenmek
336 appointment ... randevu
336 keep an appointment ... randevuya gitmek
336 hurry ... acele/acele etmek

336 take your time ... acele etmeyin
336 plenty of ... bol miktarda

LESSON 65

338 for ... -dır/-dir
338 since ... -den beri
338 period ... dönem
338 point ... nokta
339 kitchen ... mutfak
339 fridge ... buzdolabı
339 freezer ... dondurucu
339 cooker ... ocak
339 sink ... eviye
339 microwave ... mikro dalga
339 studies ... çalışmalar
340 lend - lent - lent ... borç vermek/ödünç vermek
340 return ... iade etmek
340 first name ... ilk isim
340 surname ... soyadı
340 actor ... aktör
340 actress ... aktris
340 famous ... ünlü
340 film star ... film yıldızı
341 industrial ... endüstriyel
341 agricultural ... tarımsal
341 region ... bölge
341 apologize ... özür dilemek
341 apology ... özür
341 keep somebody waiting ... birisini bekletmek
341 avoid ... kaçınmak
341 bend ... eğilmek
342 century ... yüz yıl
342 fashion ... moda
342 gate ... bahçe kapısı
342 worry ... endişelenmek
342 be worried ... endişeli olmak
342 run ... koşmak

LESSON 66

344 I was speaking ... konuşuyordum
344 particular ... belirli
344 while ... iken
345 earn ... kazanmak
345 formal ... resmi
345 informal ... gayri resmi
345 jeans ... kot
345 trainer ... spor ayakkabısı
345 how do you do? ... tanıştığımıza memnun oldum (resmi dilde)
346 persuade ... ikna etmek
346 hairdresser ... kuaför
346 so = very ... çok
346 interesting ... ilginç
346 exciting ... heyecan verici
346 grammatically ... dil bilgisi açısından
346 bathroom ... banyo
346 bath ... banyo
346 shower ... duş/sağanak
346 toilet ... tuvalet
346 basin ... küvet
347 mirror ... ayna
347 reflect ... yansıtmak
347 active ... etkin
347 passive ... edilgen
347 subject ... konu
347 object ... nesne
348 by ... tarafından

LESSON 67

350 force ... zorlamak
350 make somebody do ... birisine ... yaptırmak
350 snack ... çerez
350 break ... mola
350 biscuit ... bisküvi
350 crisps ... cips
350 to be born ... doğmak
351 murder ... cinayet
351 prison ... hapishane
351 pupil ... öğrenci
351 root ... kök
351 memory ... hafıza
352 cross ... karşıya geçmek
353 think of ... düşünmek
353 safe ... güvenli
353 safety ... emniyet
353 on your own ... kendi başınıza
353 lay ... to lie=uzanmak' fiilinin geçmiş zaman hali
354 sir ... bayım
354 madam ... bayan
354 gentleman ... beyefendi
354 lady ... hanımefendi
354 customer ... müşteri
354 officer ... memur
354 title ... ünvan
355 standard ... standart
355 height ... boy
355 colourful ... renkli

LESSON 68

356 would you say ... söyleyebilecek miydiniz
356 opinion ... fikir
357 get in ... arabaya binmek
357 get out of ... arabadan inmek
357 get on ... Otobüse/trene/uçağa/gemiye binmek
357 get offOtobüsten/trenden/uçaktan/gemiden inmek
357 taxi ... taksi
357 fare ... ücret
357 royal ... kraliyet
357 mud ... çamur
357 countryside ... kırsal kesim
357 crowd ... kalabalık
357 crowded ... kalabalık olmak
358 captain ... kaptan
358 team ... takım
358 wide ... geniş
358 narrow ... dar
358 flag ... bayrak
358 national ... ulusal
358 grass ... çim
358 live on ... ...ile beslenmek
359 tower ... kule
359 wet ... ıslak
359 dry ... kuru
359 threw "to throw=atmak" fiilinin geçmiş zaman hali
359 loud ... yüksek sesli
359 turn up ... sesini açmak
359 turn down ... sesini kısmak
360 myself ... kendim
360 yourself ... kendin
360 himself ... kendisi (erkek)
360 herself ... kendisi (bayan)
360 itself ... kendisi (hayvan veya nesne)
360 oneself ... kendi kendine
360 ourselves ... kendi kendimize
360 yourselves ... kendi kendinize
360 themselves ... kendi kendilerine

360 consequently .... sonuç olarak
360 protect .... korumak

LESSON 69

362 thorough .... tam
362 thoroughly .... tamamen
362 accident .... kaza
362 by accident .... tesadüfen
363 careful .... dikkatli
363 careless .... dikkatsiz
363 carefully .... dikkatli bir şekilde
363 carelessly .... dikkatsiz bir şekilde
363 own .... sahip olmak
363 carry on .... devam ettirmek
363 retire .... emekliye ayrılmak
364 prize .... ödül
364 too .... de, ... da
364 at least .... en azından
364 widely .... yaygın
364 manner .... davranış
364 pig .... domuz
365 asleep .... uykuda
365 awake .... uyanmış
365 hospital .... hastane
365 nurse .... hemşire
365 purpose .... amaç
365 in order to ....'mak için
365 so that .... bu yüzden
365 take exercise .... egzersiz yapmak
366 notice .... duyuru/ilan
366 lain .... "to lie=uzanmak" filinin 3. hali
367 point at .... parmakla bir nesneyi işaret etmek
367 point out .... göstermek
367 indicate .... belirtmek
367 grave .... mezar
368 neck .... boyun
368 flame .... alev
368 flight .... uçuş
368 soup .... çorba
368 except .... hariç

LESSON 70

369 may .... -ebilmek
369 might .... -ebilirdi
369 palace .... saray
369 parliament .... parlamento
370 arrive at .... belirli bir noktaya varmak
370 point .... nokta
370 arrive in .... bir ülkeye yada kente varmak
370 area .... alan
370 airport .... havaalanı
370 passport .... pasaport
370 café .... kafe
370 owe .... borçlu olmak
370 souvenir .... hediyelik eşya
371 pride .... gurur
371 proud .... gururlu
371 normal .... normal
371 normally .... normal olarak
371 take pride in .... gurur duymak
371 servant .... hizmetkar
372 wheel .... tekerlek
372 lorry .... kamyon
372 arrow .... ok
372 centimetre .... santimetre
372 metre .... metre
372 beard .... sakal
372 true .... Doğru
372 false .... Yanlış
372 paper (newspaper) .... gazete
372 maintain .... bakımını sağlamak
373 it takes .... sürer (zaman)
373 Ireland .... İrlanda
373 amount .... miktar
373 amount to .... etmek
373 further .... bundan başka/ilaveten
373 Sweden .... İsveç
373 in addition .... ek olarak
373 extra .... ekstra

LESSON 71

375 I had eaten .... yemiştim
376 party .... parti
376 political .... politik
377 mad .... kızgın; çok ilgili; çıldırmış
377 crazy .... çıldırmış
377 UFO .... UFO
377 copy .... kopya çekmek/tekrar etmek/kopya
378 influence .... etki
378 mouse .... fare
378 mice .... fareler
378 throat .... boğaz
378 opportunity .... fırsat
378 develop .... geliştirmek
378 industry .... sanayi
378 agriculture .... tarım
379 print .... yazdırmak
379 sand .... kum
379 beach .... sahil
379 desert .... çöl
379 bell .... zil
379 knock .... kapıyı çalmak
379 pay a visit .... Ziyaret etmek
379 ring .... zil/ zili çalmak
379 shout .... bağırmak
380 stick .... sopa
380 walking stick .... baston
380 exclamation mark .... ünlem işareti

LESSON 72

381 reason .... sebep
381 illness .... hastalık
381 tiredness .... yorgunluk
381 darkness .... karanlık
381 alone .... tek başına
382 already .... zaten/şimdiden/daha önce
382 thrown .... 'throw=atmak' fiilinin 3. hali
382 in spite of .... -e rağmen
382 despite .... -e rağmen
383 anyone .... herhangi birisi
383 someone .... birisi
383 no one (no-one) .... hiç kimse
384 borrow .... ödünç almak
384 my own .... kendi ...im
384 emphasize .... vurgulamak
384 skin .... cilt
385 wire .... kablo/tel
385 electricity .... elektrik
385 connection .... bağlantı
385 wireless .... kablosuz
385 Wi-Fi .... Kablosuz bağlantı
385 hyphen .... tire
385 boil .... kaynatmak
385 fry .... kızartmak
385 roast .... fırında pişirmek
385 brick .... tuğla
386 as well .... de , da
386 too .... de, da

386 also .... de , da /ayrıca

LESSON 73

387 I will be speaking .... konuşuyor olacağım
387 inch .... inç (2,54 cm)
387 foot .... adım (= 12 inç)
387 yard .... yarda (= 3 fit)
388 chain .... zincir
388 rise .... yükselmek
388 constantly .... sürekli olarak
389 belt .... kemer
389 hourly .... saatte bir
389 daily .... günlük
389 weekly .... haftalık
389 monthly .... aylık
389 yearly .... yıllık
390 allow .... izin vermek
390 let – let – let .... izin vermek
390 everyday .... gündelik

LESSON 74

392 anywhere .... herhangi bir yerde
392 somewhere .... bir yerde
392 not anywhere .... herhangi bir yerde değil
392 nowhere .... hiçbir yerde
393 loose .... serbest/ bol/ oynak
393 loosen .... gevşetmek
393 storm .... fırtına
393 lightning .... şimşek çakması
393 thunder .... gök gürültüsü
393 blind .... kör
393 devil .... şeytan
394 ride .... binmek (at, bisiklet)
394 cycle .... bisiklete binmek
394 may....-ebilmek (bir şeyi yapmak için izin isterken kullanılır)
394 can.....-ebilmek (bir şeyi yapmak için izin isterken kullanılır)
394 could..-ebilmek (bir şeyi yapmak için izin isterken kullanılır)
394 permission .... izin
394 catch .... tutmak; yakalamak
394 raincoat .... yağmurluk
395 cap .... şapka
395 habit .... alışkanlık
395 be in the habit of doing... yapma alışkanlığı olması
396 stranger .... yabancı (tanımadığımız kişi)
396 foreigner .... yabancı (bir başka ülkeden)
396 snowstorm .... kar fırtınası

LESSON 75

397 look like .... benzemek
397 travel .... seyahat etmek
397 journey .... seyahat
397 just .... sadece
398 of course .... tabii ki
398 nowadays .... bugünlerde
398 suffer .... muzdarip olmak
398 wish .... istek/dilek
398 exist .... var olmak
399 remind .... hatırlatmak
399 in other words .... bir başka ifadeyle
399 member .... üye
399 library .... kütüphane
399 even though .... -diği halde
399 even .... bile
399 not even .... hiç mi hiç
400 to..''e doğru, bir yer istikametine hareket ederken
400 at .... 'de, bir yerdeyken kullanırız
400 direction .... yön
400 soon .... yakında
400 at once .... hemen

LESSON 76

402 need .... ihtiyaç duymak
402 towards .... 'e doğru
402 destination .... varış yeri
403 tray .... tepsi
403 stadium .... stadyum
403 much better .... çok daha iyi
403 much more .... çok daha fazla
403 contrary .... tersi
403 fall .... düşmek
403 temperature .... sıcaklık
403 atmosphere .... atmosfer
404 tooth .... diş
404 teeth .... dişler
404 toothbrush .... diş fırçası
404 dentist .... diş hekimi
404 seem .... gibi görünmek
404 several .... birkaç
405 compose .... bestelemek/yazmak
405 be composed of .... 'den oluşmak
405 wise .... Mantıklı/akıllı
405 wisdom .... akıllılık
405 suddenly .... aniden
405 pain .... acı
406 certain .... emin
406 pass by .... önünden geçmek
406 park .... park etmek
406 car park .... oto park
406 picture .... resim

LESSON 77

409 diary .... günlük
410 character .... karakter
410 really .... gerçekten
410 ran .... 'To run=koşmak' fiilinin geçmiş hali
410 improve .... geliştirmek
410 coach .... antrenör/otobüs
411 flew .... 'To fly=uçmak' fiilinin geçmiş hali
411 wool .... yün
412 apostrophe .... kesme işareti
412 case .... durum
412 kick .... tekme atmak
413 coast .... kıyı
413 certain .... belirli
413 tire .... yorulmak

Notes

Notes